101
PROMISES
WORTH
KEEPING

NEIL ESKELIN

CREATION
HOUSE
BOOKS ABOUT SPIRIT-LED LIVING
ORLANDO, FLORIDA

Creation House
Strang Communications Company
600 Rinehart Road
Lake Mary, FL 32746
Fax: (407) 333-7100

Unless otherwise noted, all Scripture quotations
are from the New King James Version of the Bible.
Copyright © 1979, 1980, 1982 by Thomas Nelson Inc.,
publishers. Used by permission.

Scripture quotations marked NIV are from the Holy
Bible, New International Version. Copyright © 1973,
1978, 1984, International Bible Society.
Used by permission.

Creation House books are available to churches,
ministries and organizations at a volume discount.
Call 1-800-283-8494 for more information.

To Ian —
WHO DEMONSTRATES EVERY
DAY THAT A PROMISE MADE
IS A PROMISE KEPT

CONTENTS

INTRODUCTION

A SMALL BOY asked his father to take him to Baskin Robbins for ice cream after supper one evening. The father assured his son that they would go.

"Do you promise?" the boy wanted to know.

"I promise," the father replied.

Later, when the dad reneged on his commitment because of Monday night football, the boy was deeply disappointed. The father's image had been tarnished.

In every arena of life — at home, at work or at church — we are not measured by our promises but by our performance. People want to know: Is he honest? Can he be trusted? Will he keep his word?

Stone by Stone

I wish I could tell you that there is one simple promise that would produce such earth-shattering changes that none other would be necessary. Unfortunately, that's not possible. The qualities of our lives are established through a slow but certain process.

Every promise, if kept, is like placing a stone in the foundation of your life. When enough stones are laid you can build a solid, dependable structure.

How is our character built? According to the Word, "Precept must be upon precept, precept upon precept, line upon line, line upon line, here a little, there a little" (Isaiah 28:10).

Our vows are not only to ourselves and to God but to those we come in contact with every day. Bill McCartney, founder of the Promise Keepers movement, says, "When you make a promise to a brother, you declare your intentions and obligate yourself to follow through. You bind yourself to that person."

The Challenge

On these pages you will be asked to make commitments in five vital areas of your life.

1. *Promises to your family and friends.* What decisions can you make to strengthen your marriage and cement the relationships between you and those you love?

2. *Promises to your associates.* What type of commitments will produce accountability, cooperation, integrity, excellence, leadership and promote mutual trust?

3. *Promises to yourself.* How can you control your emotions, destroy negative habits and eliminate unhealthy fear? What vows will result in the development of your talent and produce personal growth?

4. *Promises to your world.* What personal commitments can you make that will strengthen your community and bring help and hope to those who are hurting?

5. *Promises to God.* The Almighty has made a covenant with you. Now it's your turn. You will be asked to make vows involving prayer, faith, finances and your future.

Many people make the mistake of believing that God's promises are automatic. No, they are conditional. He says *if* we will do our part, He will do His. God told Solomon, "If My people who are called by My name will humble themselves, and pray and seek My face, and turn from their wicked ways, then I will hear from heaven, and will forgive their sin and heal their land" (2 Chronicles 7:14).

Don't attempt to digest this book in one sitting. It's not a trip to a fast food restaurant, but a 101-course meal.

There will be some pages you may gloss over quickly. They will seem like words of congratulations for a commitment you've already made.

Other promises, however, may cause you to squirm. Take whatever time is necessary to work through the issue and make a deep-rooted resolution to change that area of your life.

Vows are not only for making but for renewing day after day. Remember, God has prepared eternity because you are a promise worth keeping.

I.

PROMISES TO MY FAMILY AND FRIENDS

I PROMISE TO KEEP MY VOWS OF MARRIAGE

A T HENRY FORD'S fiftieth wedding anniversary celebration, a reporter asked, "How do you account for your happy marriage?" Without hesitation, Ford replied that it was the same formula that made his automobile successful — "Stick to one model."

Today's appalling divorce statistics reveal much more than a crisis in marriage. Couples have faced pressures and conflicts since the snake tempted Adam and Eve. The real plight is a crisis of commitment — people don't mean what they say.

With This Ring

Every year, millions of couples stand before an altar and repeat, "For better or for worse, for richer for poorer, in sickness and in health, to love and to cherish, till death do us part." They place their hands on a Bible, exchange rings of fidelity and in some cases, seal the commitment with holy communion.

What went wrong? How could such a solemn pledge be broken as easily as a stick of wood?

Vows are not meant to be made with
fingers crossed hoping somehow
the pledge will be kept.

When the Pharisees questioned Jesus about the vows of marriage, the Lord was emphatic. He declared, "So then, they are no longer two but one flesh. Therefore what God has joined together, let not man separate" (Matthew 19:6).

What Real Men Do

Why do we keep a vow? Because we make a vow. It's not that complicated.

Steve Farrar, in his book, *Point Man,* states, "Real men don't have affairs because real men are responsible. Real men keep their commitments even when their personal needs are not being met the way they would hope; even when they are disappointed in their wives for some reason."

The pledge you make to your partner is not an ordinary contract filled with loopholes and escape clauses. It is your eternal covenant.

Husbands, love your wives,
just as Christ also loved the
church and gave Himself for her.
— Ephesians 5:25

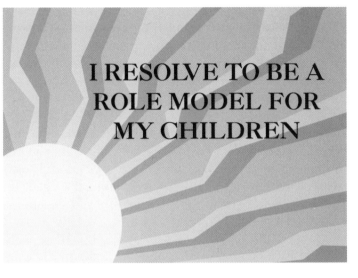

I RESOLVE TO BE A
ROLE MODEL FOR
MY CHILDREN

THE STARTLING FACT that parents ultimately discover is that children are instinctive mimics. No matter how much we tell them otherwise, they will act just like us.

The English poet John Wilmot confessed, "Before I got married I had six theories about bringing up children; now I have six children and no theories."

What is needed is not a crash course on How to Raise Great Kids but rather How to Be Great Examples.

Every mom and dad
need to see themselves
as a prototype that will
soon be reproduced.

The Die Is Cast

Good or bad, honest or deceitful, moral or immoral, we set the standard. I like what Josh Billings said: "Train up a child in the way he should go — and walk there once in a while."

What the apostle Paul told the believers at Philippi needs to be adopted by every parent: "Brethren, join in following my example, and note those who so walk, as you have us for a pattern" (Philippians 3:17).

Weaving the Fabric

The topic of family values should never be the issue of a debate. There are not two choices. We either raise children in a home with strong moral principles or we have chaos.

Ken Canfield, president of the National Center for Fathering, believes that the challenge for this generation is to make marriage a prerequisite to fathering. Says Canfield, "Every day hundreds of children are born without two parents who are committed to building a solid family together. Research confirms that these children are more likely to commit delinquent acts, drop out of school, have children out of wedlock, suffer from poverty, receive welfare, and abuse drugs and alcohol."

We may not be able to transform the world, but we will make a permanent imprint on our sons and daughters. As David Wilkerson, founder of Teen Challenge, states, "Every word and deed of a parent is a fiber woven into the character of a child which ultimately determines how that child fits into the fabric of society."

Are you the example God expects?

Train up a child in the way
he should go, and when he
is old he will not depart from it.
— Proverbs 22:6

I WILL TREASURE THE TIME I SPEND WITH MY FAMILY

IN A WORLD of two breadwinners working overtime to balance the budget and children being raised by nursery schools and babysitters, it's not surprising that parents complain, "Oh, how I wish I could spend more time with my family."

However, the question is not, What would you do if you had more time? The question is, What are you doing with the time you have?

Professional golfer Paul Azinger keeps a hectic schedule on the PGA circuit, yet he carefully carves out time for his family.

Paul says, "Your kids are only young once, and if you miss them the first time, you don't get a second chance." He adds, "When I'm home, I'm home, and I try to do things with my kids that they will always remember."

A Better Way

In many homes, the time parents spend with their

children falls under a category of the three *C*s — criticizing, correcting and controlling.

There is a better way. It involves building strong, supportive bridges to each member of your family. "I believe God intended our kids to see truth and accept it through the context of a relationship," says author and speaker Josh McDowell. "If we start teaching and don't have a relationship, we get rebellion. But if we build the relationship, those kids will die for us; they'll go to the wall for us."

Establish the habit of listening carefully to every member of your family.

*We have two ears and one mouth, so we
can listen twice as much as we speak.*

The Greatest Moments

When Jesus journeyed to Judea, parents brought their children to Him, but the disciples tried to push them away. Jesus rebuked them, saying, "Let the little children come to Me, and do not forbid them; for of such is the kingdom of God" (Mark 10:14). Then, "He took them up in His arms, laid His hands on them, and blessed them" (v. 16).

Treasure the time you spend with your family — time to listen, time to understand, time to play and time to pray. These times will be the greatest moments of your life.

*Your wife shall be like a
fruitful vine in the very heart
of your house, your children like
olive plants all around your table.*
— Psalm 128:3

I PROMISE TO MAINTAIN A CHRIST-LIKE ATMOSPHERE IN OUR HOME

EVERY HOME HAS its own unique personality you can sense the moment you walk through the front door. I've been in environments that were distant and detached and others so warm and loving that I didn't want to leave.

What makes the difference? It is not the pictures hanging on the walls or the color of the carpets, but the people who inhabit the dwelling. You don't have to wonder if the Lord is the center of the home — you can feel it!

Charles Spurgeon once said, "When a home is ruled according to God's Word, angels might be asked to stay with us, and they would not find themselves out of there element."

A United Front

Abraham Lincoln was speaking about more than a divided nation when he warned, "A house divided against itself cannot stand."

When a household is dominated by conflict, dissension and strife, everyone suffers — especially the children.

A counselor who deals with dozens of families in turmoil told me, "I have seen the disastrous results of children raised by parents with opposite temperaments; one who is over-indulgent and the other who is abusive."

Regardless of the issues that involve a son or daughter, it is imperative that both parents present an undivided, solid front. It is the natural by-product of a home where Christ is Lord.

Do you remember what Paul and Silas told the warden of the prison?

Believe on the Lord Jesus
Christ, and you will be saved,
you and your household.
— Acts 16:31

The Crown

Author Henry Van Dyke wrote, "The crown of the home is godliness; the beauty of the home is order; the glory of the home is hospitality; the blessing of the home is contentment."

Is your home built on a strong spiritual foundation? Is it filled with genuine, unconditional love? Is there open, honest communication? Is there firm, caring discipline? Are there positive models who pattern their behavior on the teachings of Christ?

But as for me and my house,
we will serve the Lord.
— Joshua 24:15

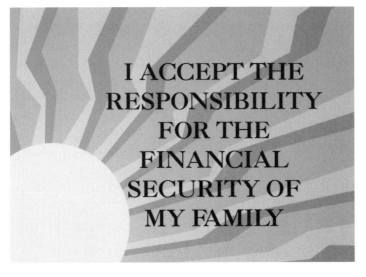

I ACCEPT THE RESPONSIBILITY FOR THE FINANCIAL SECURITY OF MY FAMILY

AS I WAS channel-surfing with my television remote control, I stopped when I saw a photo with graphics that asked, "Have you seen this man?"

On the lower part of the screen were these words: "Wanted for delinquent child support payments of $57,400." A few seconds later there was another face. The man owed $17,000. The next deadbeat dad owed $23,500.

Think of it. These men not only walked out on their families but refused to support those they had brought into this world.

The Peril of Possessions

What are parents required to provide? The three basic needs: food, shelter and clothing. That doesn't mean we must be eating gourmet dinners in a mansion and have closets filled with extravagant apparel.

We decry the alcoholic who drinks up his weekly paycheck. But we fail to recognize that millions of families live in financial crisis because of a dad who buys a luxury car he can't afford or a mother who has no self-discipline in her use of credit cards.

Don't fall in love with possessions. Don Osgood, former IBM executive, says, "A family where each one is acquiring something just for self is a bankrupt family, whether or not the money has run out. And it usually won't be long until the money runs out. If we truly love someone we are willing to deny ourselves."

You can avoid economic slavery by
understanding the difference between
needs and wants, necessities and wishes.

Your Greatest Investment

Your obligation is not only to earn what is required for the support of your family but to also manage those funds wisely. It includes both providing for today and investing in the future. The apostle Paul wrote, "Children ought not to lay up for the parents, but the parents for the children" (2 Corinthians 12:14).

Give your family the security they need — emotionally, physically and financially. It's much more than a duty; it's a joy.

But if anyone does not provide for
his own, and especially for those of
his household, he has denied the faith
and is worse than an unbeliever.
— 1 Timothy 5:8

OUR HOME WILL BE FILLED WITH JOY AND LAUGHTER

"LIGHTEN UP!" THE teacher told a distraught mom and dad who were extremely upset because their second grader was making Bs instead of As. "After all," she said, "you could have had triplets."

Many children are cheated out of their childhood by parents for whom life has become much too serious.

According to research reported by author Glen Van Ekeren, studies reveal that preschoolers laugh up to 450 times a day. What about adults? That number decreases dramatically to an average of only fifteen laughs a day — and some rarely smile at all.

How can we learn to be joyful again? The answer is obvious. Become a child once more. Don't just watch while your children are giggling, join them.

A Better Prescription

Laughter was once described as similar to changing a baby's diaper — it doesn't permanently solve any problems, but it certainly makes things more acceptable for a while. Laughter is the most inexpensive medicine ever prescribed.

Charles Schultz, the creator of *Peanuts,* observed, "If I were given the opportunity to present a gift to the next generation, it would be the ability for each individual to learn to laugh at himself."

Reasons to Smile

For an instant source of joy, open the pages of Scripture.

*God's Word is like discovering an island
of happiness in a sea of sorrow.*

Without question, the New Testament is the most uplifting book ever written. It opens with delight over the birth of Jesus and ends with a multitude singing, "Alleluia! For the Lord God Omnipotent reigns!" (Revelation 19:6).

On almost every page, even in the midst of unfortunate circumstances, there is a word of cheer. For example, after Peter and the apostles were beaten for publicly proclaiming the gospel, "they departed from the presence of the council, rejoicing that they were counted worthy to suffer shame for His name" (Acts 5:41). What did Paul and Silas do when they were thrown into prison? "At midnight [they] were praying and singing hymns to God" (Acts 16:25).

Go ahead and laugh. Fill your home with the music of the soul.

*Blessed are the people who know the
joyful sound! They walk, O Lord,
in the light of Your countenance.*
— Psalm 89:15

I WILL BRING HONOR TO MY PARENTS

"SURPRISE!" SHOUTED MARK and Brenda Jones when his parents walked into a private dining room of a restaurant in Houston.

The room was filled with relatives, friends and acquaintances — some they had not seen for decades.

Mark said, "When I learned my father had life-threatening cancer I didn't want to wait for a memorial service for people to express how much they loved my parents."

The event was like a family reunion, a milestone anniversary and a *This Is Your Life* episode all rolled into one. "It was the greatest night of our lives," said the elderly couple with tears in their eyes.

The Guarantee

God's fifth commandment is clear: "Honor your father and your mother, that your days may be long upon the land which the Lord your God is giving you" (Exodus 20:12).

It is more than a divine directive; it is an order

accompanied by a guarantee of long life. As I heard someone put it, "If we reverence old age we will *reach* old age."

Paul told the church at Ephesus, "Children, obey your parents in the Lord, for this is right. 'Honor your father and mother,' which is the first commandment with promise" (Ephesians 6:1-2).

When obedience is accompanied
by honor it brings a great reward.

What Our Esteem Reveals

Harold Brokke, in his book, *Ten Steps to the Good Life,* says this about the commandment: "Remember, the parents are not the commanders, God is! Disobedience and dishonor to parents is dishonor toward God." He adds, "Submission to parents is the first indication of submission to God."

Why do our parents deserve our highest esteem? Because they have spent a lifetime looking out for our interest, performing thousands of thankless tasks that have shaped our character.

Take a moment to consider your answer to this question: Will I be content if my children honor me in the exact same way I honor my parents?

Hopefully, your response is yes.

My son, keep your father's command, and
do not forsake the law of your mother.
— Proverbs 6:20

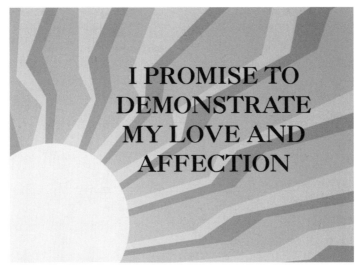

I PROMISE TO DEMONSTRATE MY LOVE AND AFFECTION

IF MY HUSBAND would only treat me like he treats our dog, Skipper, I'd be happy," a young wife told her counselor.

"What do you mean?" he asked.

"Well," she explained, "every evening when my husband comes home from work, our dog barks and rushes to him waiting for three things to happen: first, he gets a kind look; next, he gets a friendly word; and finally, Skipper gets a loving touch." She added, "I don't think that's asking too much from my husband — a look, a word and a touch."

Strong and Sensitive

In practically every nation on earth, men believe that to uphold honor they must defend their masculinity. To many people, it means being tough, rugged and as strong as steel. Some men even pride themselves in the fact that they have never shed a tear. They believe that being affectionate and caring should be delegated to the domain of the woman.

The Bible, however, tells us that men can be both strong and sensitive. King David is a good example. Do you remember how he slew a lion and a bear and was fearless in the face of Goliath?

David not only led great armies and ruled the kingdom but he also had a tender side. He had a deep love for writing poetry, and he praised the Lord with his music.

When the good Samaritan came upon the man who had been attacked by thieves, the Bible records "he had compassion" for him (Luke 10:33).

Being softhearted doesn't
mean you are soft. Being warm
doesn't mean you are weak.

Words to Rediscover

I will never forget hearing a man say, "Oh, my kids know I love them. I don't have to go around saying it all the time." He was totally wrong.

If the words *I love you,* are missing from your vocabulary, it's time to rediscover them. Scripture tells us to "Be kindly affectionate to one another with brotherly love" (Romans 12:10).

It is never too late to express the deepest feelings of your heart.

Beloved, let us love one another,
for love is of God; and everyone who
loves is born of God and knows God.
— 1 John 4:7

I WILL NEVER
HESITATE TO SAY
THANK YOU

ICOULDN'T BELIEVE it," the manager of a book store told me. "More than a year ago, my wife and I gave a gorgeous punch bowl to a young couple for their wedding, and we have yet to hear a word of thanks."

They are not alone. As a school teacher once complained, "Unfortunately, gratitude is not a topic that is included in our curriculum."

Where Were the Nine?

Even in Bible times many people were thoughtless and ungrateful. Once, when Jesus was traveling through Samaria He healed ten lepers. Were they thankful? Only one of them "when he saw that he was healed, returned, and with a loud voice glorified God, and fell down on his face at His feet, giving Him thanks" (Luke 17:15-16).

The Lord asked, "Were there not ten cleansed? But where are the nine?" (v. 17).

There is so much for which to be thankful that it's

difficult to know where to begin. We can start by saying "grace" before every meal. It is the least we can do. When Jesus fed the five thousand He gave thanks.

Boosting the Value

Every time you say *thank you,* you are increasing someone's worth. That is the definition of the word *appreciate* — to raise in value.

To maximize the effectiveness of your thanks, here are four things to remember:

1. Don't say an ordinary "Thank you." Offer one that comes from the heart and expresses your deep sincerity.

2. Speak your words of appreciation distinctly and clearly.

3. Look the person in the eyes and use their name when you thank them.

4. Recognize people for something specific they have done — not as a general response for nothing in particular.

In a world that is starved for appreciation, ask yourself, "How can I say, 'Thanks'?"

> *And let the peace of God rule in your*
> *hearts, to which also you were called*
> *in one body; and be thankful.*
> *— Colossians 3:15*

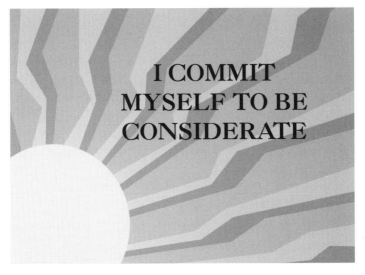

I COMMIT MYSELF TO BE CONSIDERATE

DURING THE GREAT Depression of the 1930s, Fiorello La Guardia was mayor of New York City. One night he visited a courtroom in one of the poorest sections of the city and asked the judge, "Why don't you go home for the evening and let me take over the bench?" The judge agreed.

The first case La Guardia heard that night was an elderly woman who was arrested for stealing bread. "Are you innocent or guilty?" the mayor asked.

The woman softly replied, "I needed the bread, Your Honor, to feed my grandchildren."

La Guardia responded, "I have no option but to punish you. Your sentence is ten dollars or ten days in jail."

As he proclaimed his ruling, he threw ten dollars into his hat. Then he fined every person in the courtroom fifty cents for "living in a city where a grandmother has to steal food to feed her grandchildren." When everyone contributed fifty cents, the woman paid her fine and left the courtroom with an additional $47.50.

The mayor knew the difference between correction and compassion.

How Far Will You Go?

Do your actions speak of genuine kindness and consideration? George Washington Carver believed, "How far you go in life depends on your being tender with the young, compassionate with the aged, sympathetic with the striving, and tolerant of the weak and strong. Because someday in your life you will have been all of these."

*Respect for the wishes of someone
else unlocks the door for our own
wishes to come true.*

A chemical salesman in Chicago discovered the value of being considerate. One of his customers was delighted to see him and said, "Something has just occurred to me. When other people come to my office, I say to myself, 'I wonder what they want?' but when you arrive I think, 'I wonder what he's going to do for me today?'"

The salesman was putting into practice what the apostle Paul taught long ago. "Therefore let us pursue the things which make for peace and the things by which one may edify another" (Romans 14:19). Make consideration a commitment.

*Let no one seek his own, but
each one the other's well-being.
— 1 Corinthians 10:24*

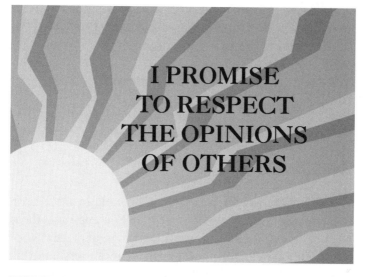

I PROMISE
TO RESPECT
THE OPINIONS
OF OTHERS

THE FOREMAN OF a manufacturing plant kept a golf ball in the top drawer of his desk. When two employees came with serious differences of opinion he would reach for the ball and hold it between the two people seated at opposite ends of his desk.

"What color is this little ball?" he asked the person on his left.

"White," was the emphatic response.

The person on the right, confused by the answer, said, "No! The ball is black."

In truth, the ball was painted black on one side and white on the other. Then the foreman told his feuding employees, "Unless you know each others' point of view, there will never be agreement on the color of the ball — or any other matter."

It was the start of a process that led to a resolution of their differences.

Understanding the opinion of someone else is essential. According to Saint Thomas Aquinas, "When you want to convert someone to your view, you go over to where he is standing, take him by the hand and guide him. You don't stand across the room and shout at him; you don't call him an idiot; you don't order him to come over to where you are. You start where he is and work from that position. That is the only way to get him to budge."

In the words of author Arthur Guitterman:

"Manner in seven words is found: Forget
yourself and think of those around."

Real Motivation

Ralph Waldo Emerson compared people to the characteristics displayed by young calves. "You can push them, pull them, prod them or even kick them, and they won't move. But give them a reason they can understand, one that will prove beneficial to them, and they will peacefully follow along."

Scripture instructs us to esteem the opinions of others — especially the wisdom of our elders. "You shall rise before the gray headed and honor the presence of an old man, and fear your God: I am the Lord" (Leviticus 19:32).

Allow your road to achievement to be paved with respect.

Honor all people. Love the brotherhood.
Fear God. Honor the king.
— 1 Peter 2:17

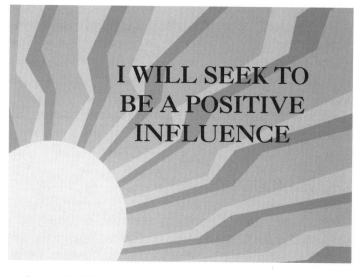

I WILL SEEK TO BE A POSITIVE INFLUENCE

A PSYCHOLOGIST GAVE ten people a series of puzzles to solve. Half were told they had done well; the other half were told they had done poorly — regardless of their actual results.

"Now I want you to try a second set of puzzles," the psychologist informed them. This time the results were different. He reported, "They did as well or as poorly as they were told they did on the first test."

The seeds you sow into those
around you will produce the fruit
you plant — whether sweet or bitter.

Mary Kay Ash, founder of the cosmetic company that bears her first names, learned how that principle operates in real life. She stated, "My experience with people is that they generally do what you expect them to do."

Dwelling on the negative simply produces more negatives. For example, Mark Tidwell, the sales manager of a

New York auto dealership maintains, "The biggest mistake you can make if cars aren't selling is to accuse your staff that it's their fault."

He explained, "I could tell them they don't know their product, they don't follow through on potential buyers or emphasize any other weakness. The more you criticize their faults, the more resentment you will produce. It won't work!"

What is the answer? Says Mark, "You have to dwell on their strengths, boost their spirits and get them motivated for the next sale."

Salt and Light

The importance of being a positive influence was addressed by the Lord when He declared, "You are the salt of the earth; but if the salt loses its flavor, how shall it be seasoned? It is then good for nothing but to be thrown out and trampled under foot by men. You are the light of the world. A city that is set on a hill cannot be hidden" (Matthew 5:13-14).

Why are we asked to let our light shine before others? It is "that they may see your good works and glorify your Father in heaven" (v. 16).

Leave the negatives to someone else. Determine that you will brighten the life of every person you touch.

And you became followers of us and of
the Lord, having received the word in
much affliction, with joy of the Holy Spirit,
so that you became examples to all in
Macedonia and Achaia who believe.
— 1 Thessalonians 1:6-7

Promise #13

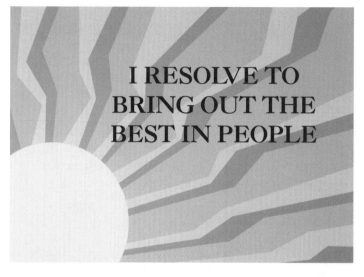

I RESOLVE TO BRING OUT THE BEST IN PEOPLE

T HE EXECUTIVE SECRETARY to a hospital administrator established a widely-known reputation for being extremely efficient. Once, she was interviewed for a company newsletter and was asked, "What's your secret for being so competent?"

She thought for a moment and replied, "Every time I do any job, no matter how insignificant, my boss applauds me so extravagantly I feel I must live up to his praise."

Searching for Gold

In my leadership seminars I have met people who shared their "war stories" of what it's like to work with someone who rules with intimidation, coercion or fear. In some cases, these seem to be the only management tools the leader has acquired. A friend who works for such an individual told me, "On most days, I get a knot in the pit of my stomach when I just *think* about going to work."

At every level of society we need people who are like

gold miners — able to extract the best in others. As writer Elbert Hubbard said, "There is something that is much more scarce, something finer, something rarer than ability. It is the ability to *recognize* ability."

Develop an attitude that
sees potential, not problems.

The need is universal. Alan Loy McGinnis, author of *The Friendship Factor,* states, "History shows that in almost every area there is a vacuum waiting to be filled by some person who can impart vision and steer people's energies into the best endeavors."

A Voice in the Storm

When Paul was a prisoner bound for Rome, the ship on which he sailed with 275 captives and their guards encountered such a violent storm that they were forced to throw much of the cargo overboard.

After many days without food, Paul brought hope to the men when he revealed what an angel told him. He stood before them and declared, "I urge you to keep up your courage, because not one of you will be lost; only the ship will be destroyed" (Acts 27:22, NIV).

You rise to new heights when you bring out the best in others.

Humble yourselves in the sight of
the Lord, and He will lift you up.
— James 4:10

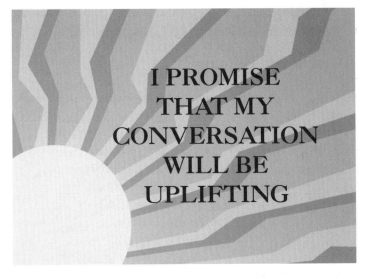

I PROMISE THAT MY CONVERSATION WILL BE UPLIFTING

MANY YEARS AGO a guest speaker at our rotary club offered a suggestion I thought I'd try. He said, "No matter what topic you may be discussing, always end the conversation on a hopeful, positive note."

That same day, I remembered his advice and gave it a try. It felt so good that I decided to make it a habit. Today I wind up virtually every meeting and every encounter with something affirmative.

One Small Push

Jean Nidetch, the founder of *Weight Watchers,* a program that has over a million members in twenty-four nations, was asked, "How have you been able to help so many people?"

She explained that her passion for helping began as a teenager. Nidetch regularly walked through the park and watched mothers chatting while their small children sat on swings with no one to push them.

"I'd give them a push," Jean recalled. "And you know what happens when you push a kid on a swing? Pretty soon he's pumping his legs, doing it himself. That is what my role in life is — I'm there to give others a push."

Remarkable Benefits

Words that edify and uplift are more than good suggestions — they are God's method of communication.

Do not let any unwholesome talk
come out of your mouths, but only
what is helpful for building others
up according to their needs, that it
may benefit those who listen.
— Ephesians 4:29, NIV

What is the impact of your inspiration? Positive thinker Norman Vincent Peale stated, "Whomever you help to build up and become a better, stronger, finer person will give you his undying devotion." He added, "Build up as many people as you can. Do it unselfishly. Do it because you like them and because you see possibilities in them. Do them good and their esteem and affection will flow back toward you."

Get in the building business. Choose constructive words.

Let the words of my mouth and
the meditation of my heart be
acceptable in our sight, O Lord,
my strength and my Redeemer.
— Psalm 19:14

Promise #15

I WILL AVOID HARMFUL CRITICISM

A S A FAVOR to some friends, my wife and I attended a fundraising dinner designed to raise money for a social service agency. Unfortunately, the large dining room was only one-third full and the embarrassed master of ceremonies was apologizing for the no-shows.

After the dinner, as we were leaving, I couldn't help overhearing the rather upset president of the organization chiding the chairman of the event, "What happened? This place would have been packed if you knew how to promote it!"

I thought, "This isn't the place for that conversation, and surely he could have found a more positive way to express his feelings."

First Things First

Certainly we have to deal with undesirable behavior, but *real* professionals use methods of correction that inspire rather than injure.

John Robinson, after a long career as a college and NFL football coach, states, "I never criticize a player until that player is convinced that I have total confidence in his talent." Robinson reminds the athlete that he is "almost perfect," but the time has come to work on the minor improvements that need to be made.

If someone says, "I'm telling you this for your own good," be careful. Often, it is not for *your* good but *theirs.*

The person who finds fault in others to boost his own vanity is usually suffering from low self-esteem. As one fellow observed:

"You have to be little, to belittle."

Human relations expert Les Giblin believes we should do our best to censure the act, not the person. He advises, "By pinpointing your criticism to his acts, you can actually pay him a compliment and build up his ego at the same time." He gives this example: "John, I know from past experience that this error is not typical of your usual performance."

The Pattern

What does Scripture say about the way we deal with others? We are "to be a pattern of good works...showing integrity, reverence, incorruptibility, sound speech that cannot be condemned" (Titus 2:7-8).

Remove blame and fault-finding from your list of leadership skills.

"Condemn not, and you
shall not be condemned."
— Luke 6:37

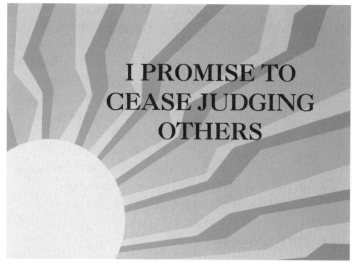

I PROMISE TO CEASE JUDGING OTHERS

THE WORLD IS filled with "Monday morning quarterbacks." They may not have the talent to compete, but they don't hesitate to offer their opinion. "How can he expect to win making stupid plays like that?"

It's been said that "one man's work is another man's target." We find self-appointed judges everywhere. For example, a world leader can make a three-minute announcement and media pundits will spend thirty hours picking over his words like buzzards descending on a dead animal.

Fighting Fire

Millions of dollars may be spent on the opening of a new Broadway show, but its success is often at the mercy of the reviews that appear in print the morning after opening night. As was said about one New York critic, "He left no *turn unstoned.*"

In many families, Sunday dinner is a weekly ritual of

pulling apart the sermon they have just heard. We need to read again the words of the apostle Paul, who proclaimed, "In whatever you judge another you condemn yourself; for you who judge practice the same things" (Romans 2:1).

People find it easy to lash out at others, but how should you react when you are the target? Don't try to fight fire with fire. It only increases the flame.

When your time is spent searching for the faults in others, you are robbing yourself of the energy it takes to accomplish God's purpose for your life.

Turn your focus inward. Self-correction
not only steers you back on course but
forces you to look in a new direction.

The Turn-Around

Instead of passing judgement, pass joy and belief. Richard De Vos, a Michigan marketing wizard, believes, "Few things in the world are more powerful than a positive push — a smile, a word of optimism and hope, a 'You can do it!' when things are tough."

God did not create us to issue rulings and pronounce verdicts. He reserves those rights for Himself. Resolve to spend your life encouraging those who are hurting and lifting those who are weak.

But why do you judge your brother?
Or why do you show contempt for your
brother? For we shall all stand before
the judgment seat of Christ.
— Romans 14:10

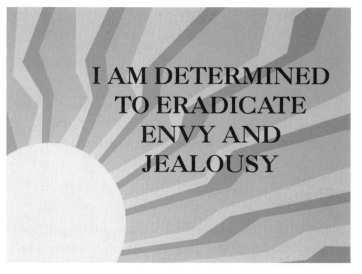

I AM DETERMINED TO ERADICATE ENVY AND JEALOUSY

A FARMER IN Tennessee had a beautiful stream flowing through his hillside field, and the land produced bountiful crops year after year. Then one day he had an argument with a neighbor who had a productive farm just below his. In a moment of jealous rage he dammed the water of the stream.

What was the result? *Both* of the farmers had a crop failure.

The behavior of people whose emotions are governed by envy or hatred often defies explanation. As I heard one man explain it, "Hating people is like burning your own house down to get rid of a rat."

Roots of Resentment

What Shakespeare called "the green-eyed monster," jealousy, still stalks the land.

- An executive finds himself seething inside

because a fellow worker was chosen over him to give a presentation at the corporation's national convention.

- A student harbors deep resentment because a lifelong friend made the basketball team and he didn't.

- A woman is overcome with envy because her neighbor's children are enrolled in a private school — something her family's budget cannot afford.

Addressing the Problem

Who is harmed when jealousy overloads your senses? You are! As one man observed, "It's like eating green apples. It doesn't make anybody sick but yourself — and you can get quite a bellyache."

Allow the Lord to cleanse your heart of this weakness before it spreads like a virus. Scripture warns, "For where envy and self-seeking exist, confusion and every evil thing are there" (James 3:16).

Remember this: jealousy indicates that you have an extremely high regard for the person that is the object of your envy. It is rarely aimed at someone you don't like.

The next time you feel a twinge of malice arising, say to yourself, "I must truly like this person. How can I demonstrate it in a positive way?"

Let us not become conceited, provoking
one another, envying one another.
— Galatians 5:26

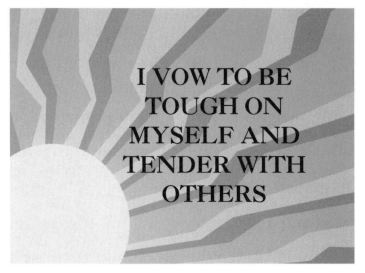

I VOW TO BE TOUGH ON MYSELF AND TENDER WITH OTHERS

SOME PEOPLE HAVE read dozens of self-help books, attended countless personal development seminars and heard hundreds of sermons on Spirit-led living, yet they still have it backwards. They attempt to rule others like a dictator — with a hand of iron and a will of steel.

How do they govern their own lives? It's just the opposite. They look for every opportunity to pamper themselves and float through life with ease.

The manager of a plastics fabrication plant was giving a tour to a group of senior citizens. One elderly gentleman asked, "How many people work here?"

The executive smiled and replied, "About half!"

Extra Effort

John D. Rockefeller was worth more than he could count, but he preached that a man has to work for his keep. He stated, "Money which comes to him without effort on his part is seldom a benefit and often a curse."

What are the rewards of self-discipline? In the words of Zig Ziglar:

"When we do more than we are
paid to do, eventually we will be
paid more for what we do."

It is not wrong to look out for your own interests, but not at the expense of others. The Bible teaches us to "See that no one renders evil for evil to anyone, but always pursue what is good both for yourselves and for all" (1 Thessalonians 5:15).

Steel and Velvet

Is it possible to be both tough and tender? According to Carl Sandburg, the famed Illinois writer, the answer is yes.

Sandburg held a joint session of Congress in the palm of his hand when he shared his eloquent thoughts about Abraham Lincoln. He said, "Not often in the story of mankind does a man arrive on earth who is both steel and velvet, who is hard as a rock and soft as drifting fog, who holds in his mind the paradox of terrible storm and peace unspeakable and perfect."

However many hats you wear, allow your life to include both strength and softness, toughness and tears.

Blessed are the merciful,
for they shall obtain mercy.
— Matthew 5:7

Promise #19

I PLEDGE THAT I WILL PRACTICE PATIENCE

IN THIS ERA of instant gratification we eat microwave meals, bank at "quick cash" automatic teller machines, develop immediate photos, fax messages to our friends and become restless if our computer can't crunch a million numbers in ten seconds.

One person looked up to heaven and prayed, "Dear Lord, please give me patience — and I want it right now!"

Persistence Pays

The great pianist Paderewski was once asked by an ardent fan, "Is it true that you still practice every day?"

"Yes," said the pianist, "at least eight hours a day."

"You must have a world of patience," the admirer added.

"I have no more patience than the next fellow," said Paderewski, "I just use mine."

At a convention in Missouri, I shared the platform with David Schwartz, the author of *The Magic of Thinking Big.* As part of his presentation, he explained there are three types of people: "Impatient, passively patient and persistently patient."

Schwartz encouraged his listeners to be in the third category — persistently patient — always working at it. "All great achievements require time," he said.

The writer of Hebrews sent the same message when he cautioned believers:

We do not want you to become lazy,
but to imitate those who through faith and
patience inherit what has been promised.
— Hebrews 6:12, NIV

It's Worth the Wait

Every farmer knows that you can't sow and reap on the same day. There is a timetable for your harvest that requires both working and waiting.

Years ago I heard a black gospel song with the title, "He May Not Come When You Want Him, but He's Right on Time." It's the story of what Job endured before being granted his ultimate reward.

Patience is a small price to pay for what you will receive someday.

And let us not grow weary while doing
good, for in due season we shall reap
if we do not lose heart.
— Galatians 6:9

I PROMISE TO
PARDON THOSE
WHO HAVE
HARMED ME

A MISSIONARY WAS captured by a group of angry men who beat him until he was almost unconscious. As he was being battered, they jeered, "What can your Christ do for you now?"

Very quietly, the missionary replied, "He can give me the strength to forgive you."

Immediately, the abuse stopped, and the men disappeared into the night.

Offering pardon is one of God's basic principles, and there are three ways to make it effective.

Pardon Promptly

What's the first thing you do at the sign of a cold or a sore throat? If you are like most people you drink some orange juice, take an aspirin and rush to the nearest pharmacy for some medication.

You take immediate action to remedy the situation because delay only makes matters worse.

The same quick response is required when we need to pardon someone for their actions against us. Every day without a resolution only multiplies the problem.

God's Word says, "Do not let the sun go down on your wrath" (Ephesians 4:26).

Pardon Peacefully

If you ever see two men with clenched fists, one thing is certain: it's impossible for them to shake hands. They need to relax and demonstrate forgiveness — what Josh McDowell calls the "oil of relationships."

Jesus proclaimed to the multitudes:

> *"Love your enemies, bless those who*
> *curse you, do good to those who hate*
> *you, and pray for those who spitefully*
> *use you and persecute you."*
> *— Matthew 5:44*

Pardon Permanently

Many people never really "bury the hatchet." Instead they build a monument to it and brag about the incident again and again. "I can forgive, but I can't forget," is only another way of saying, "I can't forgive."

With just three words you can bury the past, heal the present and open your heart to a promising future. Those words are, "I forgive you."

> *"For if you forgive men*
> *their trespasses, your heavenly*
> *Father will also forgive you."*
> *— Matthew 6:14*

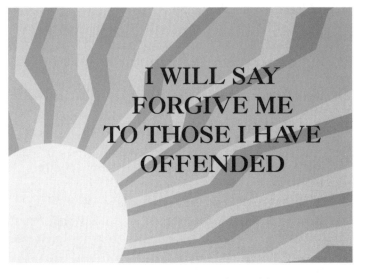

I WILL SAY FORGIVE ME TO THOSE I HAVE OFFENDED

TOM BAILEY, AN accountant in Baltimore, remembers the heated argument he had with his boss over the billing of a client. Tempers flared. Angry words were exchanged. The next morning, Tom's superior was waiting for him at the office. "Please, accept my apology for my behavior yesterday. I'm really sorry," he said.

"Don't worry about it," Tom replied, without looking up from his desk.

His boss felt much better, but Tom admits, "I was still fuming inside and couldn't bring myself to admit I was wrong."

More than two weeks lapsed before Tom realized that he also needed to apologize. Finally, he walked into the office of his superior and said, "I know this is a little late, but I'm really sorry for my outburst a couple of weeks ago. Will you forgive me?"

"Of course," replied his boss. "I forgot it immediately."

Many people find it easier to forgive others than to admit their own faults. Sales consultant Nido Qubein says,

"'Eating crow' is never pleasant — no matter how much mustard and catsup you put on it. But usually the sooner you eat it the less unpleasant it is to taste!"

To admit your failure is not an admission
of weakness but a statement of strength.

Doing Our Part

"I told him I was sorry, but he didn't accept it," a friend once lamented.

"Don't worry. You've done all that is required," I responded.

Asking forgiveness doesn't guarantee reconciliation, but it is a giant step in the right direction. It takes only one to pardon but two to reconcile. Regardless of the response, do what God requires.

Bear with each other and forgive whatever
grievances you may have against one
another. Forgive as the Lord forgave you.
— Colossians 3:13, NIV

A Requirement

Chuck Swindoll maintains, "Forgiveness is not an elective in the curriculum of life. It is a required course, and the exams are always tough to pass." The first lesson is learning to say, "Please forgive me."

Be kind and compassionate to
one another, forgiving each other,
just as in Christ God forgave you.
— Ephesians 4:32, NIV

Promise #22

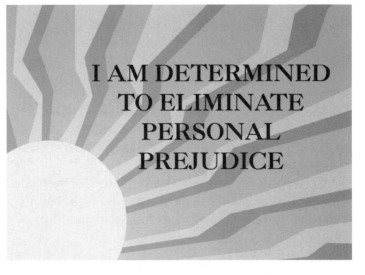

I AM DETERMINED TO ELIMINATE PERSONAL PREJUDICE

ON THE STREETS of New York City a balloon salesman knew how to attract a crowd. Before making his first sale, he took a white balloon, filled it with helium gas and it floated into the air on the string. Next, he inflated a red balloon and then a yellow one.

As children gathered around to buy his wares, a little black boy looked up at the balloons and eventually asked, "Mister, if you filled a black balloon, would it go up, too?" The man bent down and looked the boy in the eyes and said, "Of course. It's not the color of the balloon, it's what's inside that makes it rise."

Under the Surface

If the sentiment of the New York salesman was the norm rather than the exception we could eliminate one of the great scourges of our society.

Beneath the surface of a nation that claims to believe in equality is a layer of bigotry and intolerance that threatens our very foundation. It is in total contradiction to the world God created.

"He has made from one blood
every nation of men to dwell
on all the face of the earth."
— Acts 17:26

The word *prejudice* has a simple definition. It means to pre-judge — to make a decision before we know the facts. It has been demonstrated again and again that people are against what they don't understand.

An elderly man was asked what he thought of the United Nations. He replied, "I think it's a good idea, but it's a shame they have to have so many foreigners in it!"

Thumbs Down!

A survey asked respondents to check *plus* or *minus* regarding a number of cultural groups that included two fictitious names: Melonians and Waluvians. Those two names attracted a large negative vote. Why? As one participant said, "Those people sound strange. Thumbs down on them, whoever they are!"

It's time to look deep within our soul. Do we embrace all of God's creation? Do we unite rather than divide? Are we color-blind? Pray for a heart so filled with compassion that intolerance will find no place to reside.

There is neither Jew nor Greek,
there is neither slave nor free,
there is neither male nor female;
for you are all one in Christ Jesus.
— Galatians 3:28

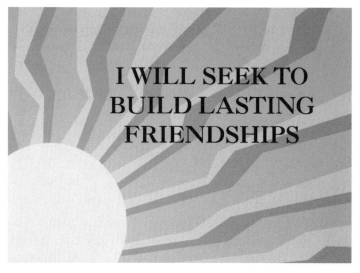

I WILL SEEK TO BUILD LASTING FRIENDSHIPS

FOR MORE THAN ten years, Frank and Steve worked in the same real estate appraisal office in Miami. When Frank was transferred to Atlanta, another colleague said to him, "I'm sure you're going to miss Steve."

"He wasn't a close friend," replied Frank, "only an acquaintance."

"But you laughed together and shared many good times," the colleague observed.

Frank paused for a moment and answered, "Yes, but we never cried together."

Who Is on the List?

If you were to compile a list of your best buddies, who would be included? Could they be counted on in a crisis? Would they still be around if your fortunes reversed?

A teacher once asked her fourth grade class to give their definition of a friend. The most insightful response was from a boy who said, "A real friend is a person who knows us and still likes us."

Your incentive to enlarge your circle of friends should have nothing to do with social status or financial reward.

We need to extend more than our hand of fellowship — we must give our heart. The Word declares:

He who loves his brother
abides in the light, and there
is no cause for stumbling in him.
— 1 John 2:10

Reaching Out

My wife and I recently had dinner with a couple who own a thriving international business. They built a large home on a lake for one purpose. "The Lord has called us to a ministry of hospitality," the husband shared. More than one thousand people from all parts of the world have visited their home. "It's what the Lord has called us to do," he explained.

They were putting into practice a rule espoused by Dale Carnegie. He said, "You can make more friends in two months by becoming interested in other people than you can in two years by trying to get people interested in you."

In the words of the telephone commercial: "Reach out and touch someone."

A man who has friends must himself
be friendly, but there is a friend who
sticks closer than a brother.
— Proverbs 18:24

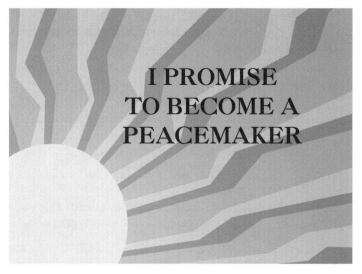

I PROMISE TO BECOME A PEACEMAKER

I REMEMBER THE day I walked into a room where two of my friends were engaged in a heated argument. If words had been bullets, I would have been ducking for cover.

To get their attention, I raised both of my hands as a signal that said, "Stop!"

When the room was finally quiet, I recalled some advice I had learned much earlier and deliberately began speaking as quietly as I could — so hushed I could barely be heard.

It worked. My friends turned down their volume and were able to discuss their differences in a civilized manner.

Centuries ago the writer of Proverbs said, "A gentle answer turns away wrath, but a harsh word stirs up anger" (Proverbs 15:1, NIV).

The Secret

Creating an atmosphere of peace and goodwill is not a complex process that requires years of strenuous study.

Stephen R. Covey, in his book, *The Seven Secrets of Highly Successful People,* says, "If I were to summarize in one sentence the single most important principle I have learned in the field of interpersonal relations, it would be this: Seek first to understand, then to be understood."

The quest for harmony and agreement is part of God's divine plan.

> *Therefore let us pursue the things*
> *which make for peace and the things*
> *by which one may edify another.*
> *— Romans 14:19*

I like the personalized license plate our friends Dave and Sally Welday placed on their Honda — 1-ACCORD.

The Right Tools

"Peace-making is a noble vocation," says Billy Graham. "But you can no more make peace in your own strength than a man can build a wall without a trowel, a carpenter build a house without a hammer or an artist paint a picture without a brush. You must have the proper equipment."

Graham added something even more crucial: "To be a peacemaker, you must know the Peace Giver. To make peace on earth you must know the peace of heaven. You must know Him who is our peace."

It's a message the world desperately needs to hear.

> *"Blessed are the peacemakers,*
> *for they shall be called sons of God."*
> *— Matthew 5:9*

I PLEDGE TOTAL
LOYALTY TO MY
FAMILY AND
FRIENDS

FOR MOST PEOPLE, loyalty doesn't have to be defined. They practice it every day. Unfortunately, their fidelity is sadly misplaced.

- Thousands of devoted Elvis fans trek to the Graceland mansion in Memphis on the birthday of "the king."

- Many sports fans will spend their last dollar to fly across the nation to cheer for their team.

- A veterinarian in Riverside, California, told me, "I have customers who are far more loyal to their dogs and cats than to members of their own family."

What has become of the devotion to our home? Where is the loyalty to those we love?

According to God's Word, our allegiance is not designed

for superstars, celebrities or dignitaries. We are to love the Lord, His church, our families and our friends.

Do you recall what happened after David killed Goliath? King Saul became jealous of David's popularity and tried to have him killed. Saul's son, Jonathan, however, defended David, and their bond of friendship never died.

Jonathan said to David, "Go in peace,
for we have a sworn friendship with each
other in the name of the Lord."
— 1 Samuel 20:42, NIV

An Alarming Price

Disloyalty takes a dreadful toll. We only have to look at the life of the disciple Judas to see the horrible consequences. After he betrayed Christ for thirty pieces of silver, Judas was so overcome with guilt and remorse that he took his own life.

True faithfulness endures storms, withstands enticement and does not flinch when under attack. For example, although Daniel landed in the lions' den, he remained loyal to his commitment to God over King Darius (Daniel 6).

You're only going to live once. Make a pledge to demonstrate your loyalty to your family, your friends and those who deserve your trust.

"Greater love has no one than this, than to
lay down one's life for his friends."
— John 15:13

II.

PROMISES TO
MY ASSOCIATES

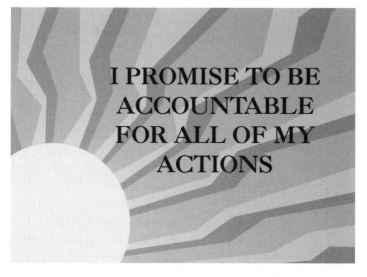

I PROMISE TO BE ACCOUNTABLE FOR ALL OF MY ACTIONS

THE MIAMI DOLPHINS set a modern NFL record during their undefeated season in 1972 that led to a Super Bowl championship. I was a postgraduate student at the University of Miami that year and had the chance to watch the historic team. Coach Don Shula produces winners because he preaches that each athlete must accept total responsibility for every action. He states, "The superior man blames himself. The inferior man blames others."

A Moment of Rage

Do you remember the story of Cain and Abel? They each brought gifts to the Lord, but God was not pleased with Cain's offering — perhaps because his heart was not right. Instead of asking for forgiveness, Cain became angry with God and with his brother, Abel.

One day, when they were out in the field together, Cain, in a fit of jealousy, struck Abel and killed him.

"Where is Abel, your brother?" the Lord asked.

Cain answered, "I do not know. Am I my brother's keeper?"

He refused to take responsibility for his action and was expelled from Eden.

There's No Escape

Just before Jesus was crucified, Pilate had second thoughts about his involvement in the matter. During the Feast that was taking place at the time it was a custom to release one prisoner chosen by the crowd. "Who should I release?" asked Pilate. "Barabbas or Jesus?"

The people shouted, "Give us Barabbas."

Scripture records that "Pilate saw that he could not prevail at all, but rather that a tumult was rising, he took water and washed his hands before the multitude, saying, 'I am innocent of the blood of this just Person. You see to it'" (Matthew 27:24).

Who is ultimately accountable for your behavior? Your parents? Your associates? Your Creator? No. The obligation cannot be shifted. You must give the final answer.

Bishop Fulton J. Sheen wrote, "Life is like a cash register in that every account, every thought, every deed, like every sale, is registered and recorded."

Don't wait for the final judgment. Accept personal responsibility now.

So then each of us shall give
account of himself to God.
— Romans 14:12

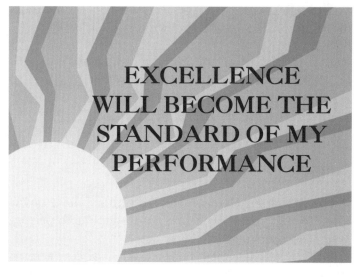

EXCELLENCE WILL BECOME THE STANDARD OF MY PERFORMANCE

IT'S COMING IN the doors," H. L. Mencken, writer and long-time publisher of *American Mercury* magazine, shouted to his employees.

Everyone ceased what they were doing and looked at the boss. "It's up to the bottom of the desk," he exclaimed. "It's up to the seat of our chairs!"

"What are you talking about?" demanded one of his bewildered colleagues.

Mencken continued, "It's all around us. Can't you see it?" He jumped up on the top of his desk.

Others in the newsroom asked, "What do you mean?"

Mencken loudly replied, "Mediocrity! We're drowning in mediocrity!"

Immediately the publisher left the building and allowed his stunned employees to reflect on his statement.

Mencken refused to be affiliated with any organization that didn't strive for excellence. He also made certain that those around him knew how much he despised inferior performance.

What about you? How strong is your commitment to the highest of standards?

The call to quality and perfection has echoed through the centuries. The apostle Paul wrote:

> *And this I pray, that your love may*
> *abound still more and more in knowledge*
> *and all discernment, that you may approve*
> *the things that are excellent.*
> *— Philippians 1:9-10*

Only the Best

Would you board a commercial airline with a novice pilot? Would you allow a surgeon-in-training to perform your heart operation? Of course not.

In His Sermon on the Mount, Jesus declared, "Therefore you shall be perfect, just as your Father in heaven is perfect" (Matthew 5:48).

Sometimes 99.9 percent accuracy isn't good enough. We need perfection. Perhaps that's why the best parachute folders are those who jump themselves.

Excellence needs to become more than our goal; it should be our pattern. As Ralph Waldo Emerson said, "Do nothing ordinary."

> *But earnestly desire the best gifts. And*
> *yet I show you a more excellent way.*
> *— 1 Corinthians 12:31*

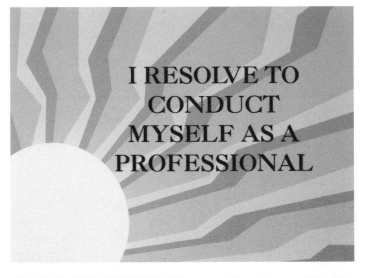

I RESOLVE TO
CONDUCT
MYSELF AS A
PROFESSIONAL

TOM DEMPSEY WAS born without toes on his right foot, yet his parents refused to pamper him because of his disability. Instead of using crutches, he was encouraged to walk the best he could and never make excuses.

Not only did he walk but he became an outstanding athlete — a *professional* athlete.

They still talk about Dempsey in New Orleans where he was a place kicker for the Saints. Tom's sixty-three-yard field goal in a game against the Detroit Lions still stands as the longest field goal in NFL history.

Total Effort

I have yet to hear of a master craftsman, an opera star or a gifted actor who reached the top without training and practice. For example, Charles Dickens didn't become a great writer by some fluke. He stated, "Whatever I have tried to do in my life, I have tried with all my heart to do well. What I have devoted myself to, I have devoted myself to completely."

God expects you to be self-reliant. Here's what the apostle Paul told the believers at Galatia:

> *But let each one examine his own work,*
> *and then he will have rejoicing in himself*
> *alone, and not in another. For each one*
> *shall bear his own load.*
> *— Galatians 6:4-5*

A Better Idea

Don't focus on your handicaps; put the spotlight on your skills.

Thomas Edison was hard of hearing, but he didn't spend all of his time trying to improve his listening skills. Instead, he concentrated on his talent to organize, to think and to create. What was the result? The great inventor held over thirteen hundred patents including the phonograph, the incandescent lamp and the electric railroad.

How would you rank your effort to be the best? Fair? Good? Superior?

On the back of a training manual for an insurance company was printed these words: "Being a professional is knowing how to do it, when to do it and doing it."

> *Therefore, brethren, be even more diligent*
> *to make your call and election sure, for if*
> *you do these things you will never stumble.*
> *— 2 Peter 1:10*

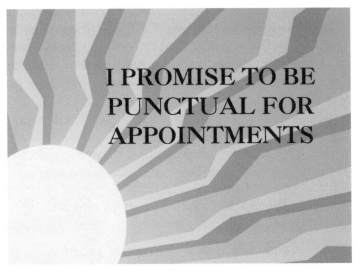

I PROMISE TO BE PUNCTUAL FOR APPOINTMENTS

HOW WOULD YOU feel if you had dinner reservations and your invited guest failed to show up on time? Has this happened to you? Ten minutes pass, then fifteen minutes and so on. Before you know it, you realize you've waited thirty minutes, and you've looked at the menu so much you can order your dinner by memory.

Now put the shoe on the other foot. What is your reputation for promptness and punctuality? Have there been times when your friends and associates thought your watch had stopped?

Manufacturing plants across the nation have adopted a "just in time" production schedule where all the parts arrive exactly when they are needed. In many cases it has totally eliminated the need for inventory warehouses. It would be great if employees embraced the same philosophy of adhering to a precise timetable.

Where's the Doctor?

A sales manager told his associates, "I won't let a doctor or dentist keep me waiting long. I will wait fifteen minutes. Then I go to the receptionist and say, 'Is the doctor ready to see me? My appointment was for three o'clock. If he can't, I will have to reschedule because I have pending appointments.'"

What happens? The manager added, "They will usually find a way to fit me in immediately."

Regardless of your occupation or status in life, it doesn't pay to be habitually late. Here are three reasons why:

1. It demonstrates a lack of consideration for others.

2. It communicates a shortage of personal organization.

3. It damages your reputation.

Wake Up!

Our heavenly Father keeps His schedule and so should we. The apostle Paul wrote, "It is high time to awake out of sleep; for now our salvation is nearer than when we first believed" (Romans 13:11).

Make punctuality your password. If you schedule an appointment, be there — even if the other person is late.

Also, learn the importance of *leaving* on time. Your minutes are too valuable to waste.

> *I made haste, and did not delay*
> *to keep our commandments.*
> *— Psalm 119:60*

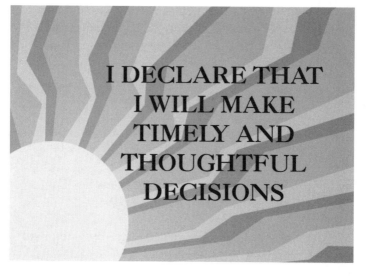

I DECLARE THAT I WILL MAKE TIMELY AND THOUGHTFUL DECISIONS

AN EXECUTIVE ADMITTED he had problems making decisions, and it was keeping him from advancing professionally. His boss made an appointment for him to see a psychiatrist.

During their first meeting, the specialist asked, "I understand you're having trouble with decision-making. Is that true?"

The man looked at the psychiatrist for a moment and hesitatingly replied, "Well, yes — and no!"

As a woman in Minneapolis who owns a greeting card shop stated, "I need to add a third tray next to the ones marked 'In' and 'Out' — one called 'Stalled.'"

Daily Dilemmas

In reality, we all have a greater capacity to make timely and thoughtful choices than we might believe. If not, how could we survive the daily drive home through rush hour traffic? It takes hundreds of instant decisions.

Since experience is the best teacher, most of our responses become automatic. Economist Marion Folson says, "You are going to find that 95 percent of all decisions you'll ever make in your career could be made as well by a reasonably intelligent high school sophomore. But they'll pay for the other five percent."

Is It Right?

What do most experts advise about resolving an issue? Don't hesitate. Take action.

A wrong decision is better than no decision; at least it can be corrected.

How can you have confidence that your judgment is right? A woman who serves on an arbitration panel said, "I use the universal approach. I ask myself, 'What if my decision were adopted by every person in the world? Would it be good for everybody or bad?'"

John Mott, president of a travel company, told his employees, "If you want to make decisions, then eliminate all the alternatives with the power of factual data. If you do not want to make decisions, then do us all a favor by staying out of the way." Decide to decide.

Therefore, when I was planning this, did I do it lightly? Or the things I plan, do I plan according to the flesh, that with me there should be Yes, Yes, and No, No? But as God is faithful, our word to you was not Yes and No...but in Him was Yes.
— 2 Corinthians 1:17-19

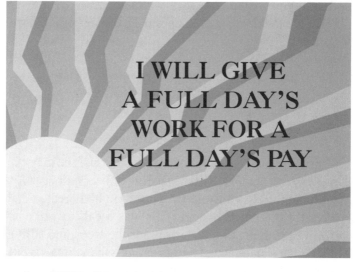

I WILL GIVE A FULL DAY'S WORK FOR A FULL DAY'S PAY

AFTER SCHOOL ONE day, three boys were bragging about their father's abilities. The first boy boasted, "My dad is so fast he can shoot an arrow at a target and catch the arrow before it even reaches the target."

The second boy responded, "That's pretty good, but my dad is so fast he can shoot at a deer and tackle the deer before the bullet gets there."

The third boy listened quietly, and then he said, "My dad is faster than both of yours. He can get off work at 4:30 and be home by 4:15!"

It's the Law!

Can you imagine the incredible production of an organization whose employees actually did what they were paid to do?

We were not created to waste our time on trivial pursuits. Work is so important that God included it in the Ten

Commandments: "Six days you shall labor and do all your work, but the seventh day is the Sabbath of the Lord your God. In it you shall do no work" (Exodus 20:9-10).

What are the dangers of idleness? The writer of Proverbs declares:

> *He who tills his land will be satisfied with*
> *bread, but he who follows frivolity is*
> *devoid of understanding.*
> *— Proverbs 12:11*

Chuck Colson and Jack Eckerd, in their insightful book, *Why America Doesn't Work,* make this observation: "God called mankind to cultivate the world He had created and to exercise dominion over it. This was a call to work, to perform both manual labor (pruning the trees and tilling the fields) and intellectual labor (naming the animals); one was not set above the other as greater or more important — a mistake frequently made by subsequent generations."

The Bottom Line

We need to continually ask ourselves, "Am I really doing what is expected of me? Do I truly earn my keep?"

It is vital that our answer be yes.

> *In all labor there is profit, but idle*
> *chatter leads only to poverty.*
> *— Proverbs 14:23*

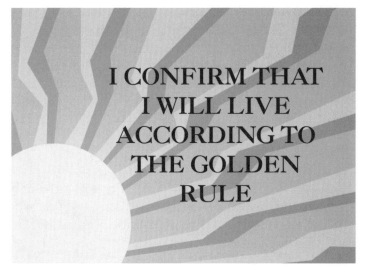

I CONFIRM THAT I WILL LIVE ACCORDING TO THE GOLDEN RULE

A LIFE INSURANCE salesman in Chattanooga, who led his company for years, was asked his secret for such great success. "Mentally," he said, "I place myself in the seat of the buyer. I determine their needs and wants. I don't sell products, I fulfill desires and give the same service I would want for myself."

The salesman was putting into practice what has been called the Golden Rule: "Do unto others as you would have others do unto you." It is considered by many to be the highest rule of life.

Affirmative Action

Several ancient Greek and Jewish leaders taught this concept in the negative form. For example, Isocrates wrote in the third century B.C., "Do not do to others what angers you if done to you by others."

When Christ walked the earth, His message was positive. Jesus declared, "Therefore, whatever you want men to do to you, do also to them, for this is the Law and the Prophets" (Matthew 7:12).

If you were having a picnic at the lake and saw a fisherman drowning after falling out of his rowboat, how would you respond? I believe you would immediately jump into the water and try to save the life of the stranger. Why? First, because you see someone in need; and second, you hope that if you were in a similar situation, someone would swim to your rescue.

The Key Word

I was disturbed when I heard someone say, "The only Christmas cards I'm sending this year are to those who send me one first." That is not the spirit of Christmas.

The key word of the Golden Rule is "Do."
In other words, the first step is yours.

Don't listen to those who say, "Do others before they do you!" Weeds and flowers live by the law of sowing and reaping. If you want to reap something beautiful, that is what must be planted.

In your heart you know what is right. Now demonstrate it in your life.

"Judge not, and you shall not
be judged. Condemn not, and
you shall not be condemned.
Forgive, and you will be forgiven."
— Luke 6:37

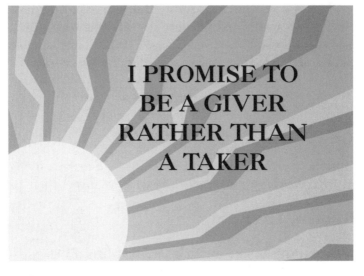

I PROMISE TO BE A GIVER RATHER THAN A TAKER

ACCORDING TO ANCIENT Roman law, a soldier had the right to ask any passerby to carry his pack for one mile. A tired warrior once asked an old man to carry his load. At the end of the mile the old man refused to put down his burden.

"You have carried it for a mile," insisted the soldier. "Please put it down. I can carry it now."

"I don't want to put it down," replied the old man. "Let me explain. The first mile is an obligation to my country, but if I am to be of real service, I must go beyond my duty. That is why I want to carry it a second mile."

Your True Value

The decision to be a giver rather than a taker produces a new perspective on life.

"May I ask how much you are worth?" a reporter asked a very wealthy man.

"$400,000," he replied.

"But according to our sources you have several million dollars in assets," the journalist retorted.

"That's true," the man said. "But you asked me how much I was worth, and I believe my worth is what I give, not what I possess. Last year I gave $400,000 to charitable causes, and to me that is the barometer of my true worth."

If your assets were based on your giving rather than your resources, what would your value be?

In the words of Winston Churchill, "We make a living by what we get; we make a life by what we give."

Running Over

Generosity is like a rising tide that lifts all ships — everybody benefits. The Chinese have a saying worth remembering: "An essence of fragrance always clings to the hand of the one who gives the rose."

A spirit of charity is not an option but a divine directive. When Jesus sent out the twelve disciples, He told them, "Freely you have received, freely give" (Matthew 10:8). Start giving today.

"Give, and it will be given to you: good measure, pressed down, shaken together, and running over will be put into your bosom. For with the same measure that you use, it will be measured back to you."
— Luke 6:38

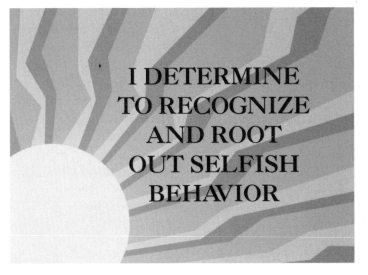

I DETERMINE TO RECOGNIZE AND ROOT OUT SELFISH BEHAVIOR

I'M NOT AGAINST anybody; I'm just for myself," said a Texas college student when members of his fraternity chided him for being uncaring and self-centered.

He is not alone. Millions of people are caught up in this dangerous view. Psychologist James Dobson has said, "The philosophy of 'me first' has the power to blow our world to pieces, whether applied to marriage, business, or international politics."

Scripture warns us we will be faced with such beliefs at the end of the age. "For men will be lovers of themselves, lovers of money, boasters, proud, blasphemers, disobedient to parents, unthankful, unholy" (2 Timothy 3:2). That day has arrived.

Bigger Barns

Once, when Jesus was teaching, someone in the crowd said to him, "Teacher, tell my brother to divide the inheritance with me" (Luke 12:13, NIV).

The Lord used the opportunity to convey a parable about the dangers of selfishness. He told about a wealthy man whose crops were so plentiful that he decided to build bigger barns. The man said to himself, "You have plenty of good things laid up for many years. Take life easy; eat, drink and be merry" (v. 19).

"But God said to him, 'You fool! This very night your life will be demanded from you. Then who will get what you have prepared for yourself?'" (v. 20).

Here is the Lord's warning:

> *"Watch out! Be on your guard against all*
> *kinds of greed; a man's life does not consist*
> *in the abundance of his possessions."*
> *— Luke 12:15, NIV*

What Is Our Score?

If you asked ten close friends to rate your behavior on a scale of one (self-centered) to ten (others-centered), what would your ranking be?

Perhaps we need to take our cue from insects. Flies, which live to satisfy their own interest, live in the dust and eat from the rubbish. Bees, however, with their desire to serve mankind with sweetness and honey, have been given the right to nourish themselves on the nectar of flowers. Allow your life to blossom. Root out selfish behavior.

> *For to me, to live is Christ,*
> *and to die is gain.*
> *— Philippians 1:21*

I PROMISE NEVER TO SEEK REVENGE

IN KANSAS, A teenager was offended by the man who owned the farm next to where his family lived. To get revenge, the young man went to a nearby agricultural supply store and bought some Johnson grass seed — a very obnoxious grass that is almost impossible to get rid of once it spreads.

In the middle of the night the boy sowed his neighbor's land with this horrible seed. Before long the grass came up and greatly damaged the farm.

About four years later the young man fell in love with the neighbor's daughter and married her. Later, the farmer died and willed the acreage to his daughter. For thirty years the man has been fighting Johnson grass — reaping what he had sown.

Getting Even?

Some people spend a lifetime attempting to retaliate for a perceived wrong. Unfortunately, it robs them of their energy, misplaces their focus and keeps them from accomplishing anything worthwhile.

Perhaps you've heard someone say, "I've been waiting ten years to get even with him." Or, "She double-crossed me once, and I will make her regret it if it takes the rest of my life!" People who utter such phrases are really saying, "I'm a little person."

History tells us that great achievers have almost always refused to yield to vindictiveness and hate.

The Chicago columnist, Sidney Harris, wrote, "When we 'get even' with someone, that is literally what we are doing — becoming even with them; that is, descending to their level in vengeance and losing whatever moral advantage we may have had."

Turning the Other Cheek

Listen to the Lord's message on vengeance. He declared, "You have heard that it was said, 'You shall love your neighbor and hate your enemy.' But I say to you, love your enemies, bless those who curse you, do good to those who hate you, and pray for those who spitefully use you and persecute you" (Matthew 5:43-44). Don't seek revenge; seek peace.

> *If your enemy is hungry, give him*
> *bread to eat; and if he is thirsty,*
> *give him water to drink.*
> *— Proverbs 25:21*

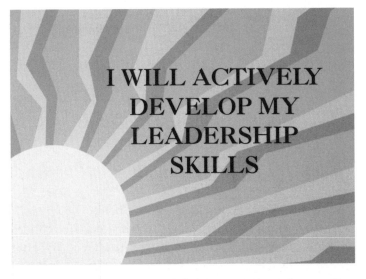

I WILL ACTIVELY DEVELOP MY LEADERSHIP SKILLS

FOR SEVERAL YEARS I have presented a seminar titled *Leaders Are Lovers*. The theme is simple: If you want rabbits to move, carrots work better than sticks.

Many people still believe the objective of leadership is one of control. They study how to take charge of time, finances, physical resources and how to control people.

Fortunately, we're discovering that the more we attempt to control others, the more they balk and rebel. Outstanding executives don't seek to domineer, intimidate or overregulate. Instead, they seek to empower and enable others to achieve.

Traits at the Top

We often envision the leader of the pack as an extrovert with a dynamic, energetic, intense personality. Those may be desired qualities, but leaders who last also have strong purpose, belief and integrity. What they do is more important than what they say.

- Real leaders are not aloof but approachable.

- Real leaders are not cold but caring.

- Real leaders are not tied to policies but to people.

- Real leaders are not dogmatic and inflexible but are open to new ideas.

Leadership is not a title or a position; it is a dynamic process.

The Flock and the Shepherd

Wess Roberts in his fascinating book, *Leadership Secrets of Attila the Hun,* states, "Without a flock there can be no shepherd. Without an army there can be no battle captains. Without subordinates there can be no leaders. Leaders are, therefore, caretakers of the interest and well-being of those and the purposes they serve."

It is also vital that we recognize the source of our wisdom and guidance: the great Shepherd. The psalmist wrote, "Lead me in our truth and teach me, for You are the God of my salvation; On You I wait all the day" (Psalm 25:5).

Instead of following a path, create one. Instead of copying someone's vision, discover your own. Leaders lead.

I will bring the blind by a way they did not know; I will lead them in paths they have not known. I will make darkness light before them, and crooked places straight. These things I will do for them, and not forsake them.
— Isaiah 42:16

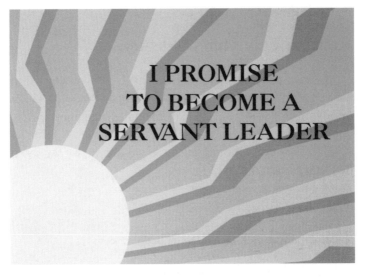

I PROMISE TO BECOME A SERVANT LEADER

PAUL "BEAR" BRYANT, the legendary football coach at the University of Alabama, knew the secret of leading men to great achievement.

He once observed, "I'm just a plowhand from Arkansas. But I have learned how to hold a team together, how to lift some men up, how to calm down others, until finally they've got one heartbeat together — a team. There are just three things I'd ever say:

'If anything goes bad, *I* did it.

If anything goes semi-good, then *we* did it.

If anything goes real good, then *you* did it.'"

Bryant added, "That's all it takes to get people to win football games for you."

Coercion Doesn't Work

We may be able to herd sheep and drive cattle, but those methods backfire with people. In the short run there may be progress attributed to force or intimidation, but it will never last. The only leadership that prevails is based on love and mutual respect.

We're in This Thing Together

In Japan there is a well-known saying: "We all eat from the same pot." It's true. If the bowl becomes empty, everyone from the shipping clerk to the sales manager and the company president goes hungry.

What a world it would be if everyone lived by the motto of Rotary International:

"Service above self."

The Surefire Path to Greatness

Questions of rank and status have no place in the Lord's value system.

When James and John asked for special seats of honor, Jesus called the disciples together and said, "You know that those who are regarded as rulers of the Gentiles lord it over them, and their high officials exercise authority over them. Not so with you. Instead, whoever wants to become great among you must be your servant, and whoever wants to be first must be slave of all" (Mark 10:42-44, NIV).

Servant leadership works — in reaching objectives, in building relationships and in receiving God's approval. It's a commitment worth making.

> *"Well done, good and faithful servant;*
> *you have been faithful over a few things,*
> *I will make you ruler over many things."*
> *— Matthew 25:23*

Promise #38

I COMMIT TO SEEK COOPERATION NOT COMPETITION

THE VICE PRESIDENT of a manufacturing plant was asked to discuss his personal best. He paused for a few moments and said, "I can't tell you about my personal best."

When asked why, he replied, "Because it wasn't me. It was *us.*"

Creating competition between team members rarely works. In fact, it's often a destructive force that makes more enemies than friends. Can you really expect ten car salesmen to get along when they are each trying to win a trip to Bermuda by making top salesman of the month!

It's Not a Contest

My friend Charles Dygert, author of *Success Is a Team Effort,* states, "You don't have to excel in every area to be a success. If there is a gap in your skills, you can join forces with others to add even greater strength. When you form a team, it's amazing how the power multiplies."

God placed you on this earth to create not to compete. Cooperation works because comparable goals promote trust, encourage communication and decrease the fear of exploitation. Leaders in business, government and education are discovering that if we compete internally, we can't successfully compete externally.

Rebuilding the Wall

One of my favorite books by Chuck Swindoll is titled *Hand Me Another Brick.* It's the story of how Nehemiah led the people to rebuild the walls of Jerusalem. Says Swindoll, "The first thing Nehemiah did was unify the people around the same goal."

The goal was preservation. Nehemiah wrote that "half of my servants worked at construction, while the other half held the spears, the shields, the bows, and wore armor; and the leaders were behind all the house of Judah. Those who built on the wall, and those who carried burdens, loaded themselves so that with one hand they worked at construction, and with the other held a weapon" (Nehemiah 4:16-17).

Build your future on the foundation of cooperation.

"Agree with your adversary quickly,
while you are on the way with him, lest
your adversary deliver you to the judge,
the judge hand you over to the officer,
and you be thrown into prison."
— Matthew 5:25

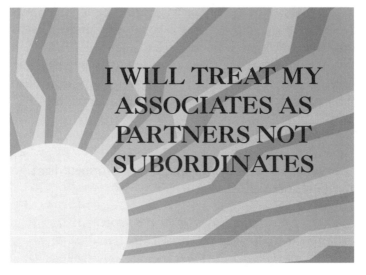

I WILL TREAT MY ASSOCIATES AS PARTNERS NOT SUBORDINATES

ALEXANDER THE GREAT, the Greek king, once led his troops across a hot, arid desert. After nearly two weeks of marching, he and his soldiers were near death from thirst, but Alexander pushed ahead.

In the noonday sun, two of his scouts brought what little water they were able to find. It barely filled a cup. Alexander's troops were shocked when he poured the water into the burning sand.

The king said, "It is of no use for one to drink when many thirst."

Alexander was a great leader because he treated his troops as equals, not as servants or slaves.

You Hold the Key

Treating those who report to you as your partners or associates will not work if it's only a scheme or a strategy. It must be a genuine heart-felt expression. The writer of Proverbs echoed that sentiment when he wrote, "Do not withhold good from those to whom it is due, when it is in the power of your hand to do so" (Proverbs 3:27).

The owner of a computer software company who was lauded by his employees was asked to explain his leadership style. "All shoes fit me!" He exclaimed. "If I am in any situation involving someone else, I try to put myself in the other fellow's shoes. I try to see things as he sees them and realize there is another viewpoint besides my own."

Surprising Strength

If you want to watch people be transformed, learn to give high appraisals.

A surefire way to motivate people to exceed their own expectations is to grade them higher than they grade themselves.

When we truly believe in the potential of people, they rarely disappoint us. That is one of the messages of Max DePree, in his perceptive book, *Leadership Is an Art.* He recommends becoming "abandoned to the strengths of others — of admitting that we cannot *know* or *do* everything."

Remarkable things transpire in an atmosphere of equality. Create a partnership.

Let nothing be done through selfish ambition or conceit, but in lowliness of mind let each esteem others better than himself.
— Philippians 2:3

I PROMISE TO PROMOTE MUTUAL TRUST

S OME PEOPLE HAVE thankless jobs and receive little support or encouragement. I smiled when I heard about what happened to a New York school superintendent.

He was rushed to the hospital for an emergency operation, and when he came out from under the anesthetic, a fax message was waiting for him. It read: "The school board voted eight to six last night to wish you a speedy recovery."

Passing the Test

You may be the most honest, straightforward and sincere person alive, but don't expect people — especially new acquaintances — to accept you with open arms. Most of us are cautious by nature and hesitate to give a quick stamp of approval. As a friend recently confided, "I've been burned too many times."

Trust is not endowed; it is *earned* as a result of

successfully passing countless small tests you may not even know you are taking.

The challenge we all face is to create an atmosphere that believes and expects only the best from others. Frank Crane, a physician, stated, "You may be deceived if you trust too much, but you will live in torment if you do not trust enough."

If you genuinely believe in people, let them know. That's what the apostle Paul did when he wrote to the church at Corinth:

> *I have said before that you have such*
> *a place in our hearts that we would live*
> *or die with you. I have great confidence*
> *in you; I take great pride in you.*
> *— 2 Corinthians 7:3-4, NIV*

Total Reliance?

You demonstrate your belief in others the way you assign tasks. I've observed leaders who give the impression they are delegating, but in reality they always hold the right to make the final decision. The message they are communicating is: "I trust you with the minor choices but not the important ones."

Express total confidence in those around you. Have faith in their wisdom, rely on their trust.

> *For by wise counsel you will wage*
> *your own war, and in a multitude*
> *of counselors there is safety.*
> *— Proverbs 24:6*

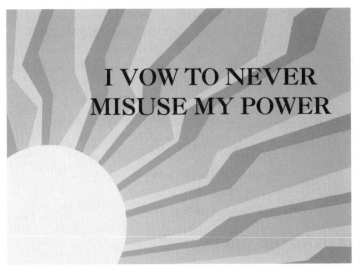

I VOW TO NEVER MISUSE MY POWER

THE OFFICE OF the U.S. presidency was shaken to its core when Richard M. Nixon resigned because of revelations that he had misused his authority.

Two decades earlier Harry Truman, commenting on the wisdom of limiting the term of the presidency to eight years, stated, "There's a lure in power. It can get into a man's blood just as gambling and the lust for money have been known to do."

Have you ever wondered how your behavior might change if you had unlimited command and control? Are you beyond temptation? Billy Graham said, "Everybody has a little bit of Watergate in him."

The Voice Inside

God has placed something within each of us that is more valuable than any computer chip — it's called a conscience. How we respond to that small inner voice can have far-reaching consequences.

People are not simply watching other's lives, they are examining them closely. The president of American Airlines, Robert L. Crandall, observed, "People want to be proud of their leaders, and that means you can't be perceived by your people as somebody likely to cheat them or cheat others, or a person whose standards they can't subscribe to."

Regardless of the level of your authority, how you use it is the result of a personal choice. The Word declares:

> *Do not withhold good from those*
> *to whom it is due, when it is in the*
> *power of your hand to do so.*
> *— Proverbs 3:27*

How Would You Decide?

Your standards must never be negotiated — even if your career is jeopardized. General Norman Schwarzkopf, who lead the Desert Storm invasion of Iraq, stated, "If it ever came to a choice between compromising my moral principles and the performance of duties, I know I'd go with my moral principles."

Is that your commitment? With God's help, you can resist even the slightest temptation to misuse your power.

> *Woe to those who devise iniquity,*
> *and work out evil on their beds!*
> *At morning light they practice it*
> *because it is in the power of their hand.*
> *— Micah 2:1*

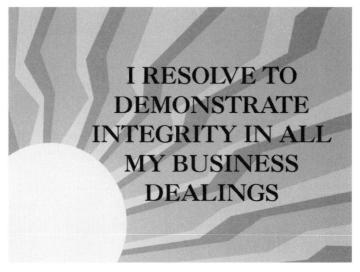

I RESOLVE TO DEMONSTRATE INTEGRITY IN ALL MY BUSINESS DEALINGS

RECENTLY *USA TODAY* reported a survey by the Ethics Resource Center. Here are the percentage of workers who say that these ethical infractions are committed by co-workers:

- Lying to supervisors — 56 percent
- Falsifying records — 41 percent
- Office theft — 35 percent

In earlier times people worried about the butcher who placed his thumb on the scales. Now an unscrupulous butcher can simply program an inflated price into the computer bar code. Our high-tech world has not changed the heart of man, only his methods of deceit.

Setting the Example

In the workplace, some leaders send mixed messages to

their people. In one breath they state, "We simply won't tolerate unprincipled activity." Then they say, "You're running behind your budget projections, and we expect you to make it. Don't tell me how you do it — just make it happen!" As author Peter Drucker states, "Ethics stays in the preface of the average business science book."

Many people assume they are getting away with their shrewd and devious ways, but they are not. Robert Noyce, the inventor of the silicon chip, observes, "I don't believe unethical people get ahead in business. If ethics are poor at the top, that behavior is copied down through the organization."

Integrity isn't measured in degrees,
you either have 100 percent or
you don't have any.

We Can't Hide

Obey God's Word on the issue. "See then that you walk circumspectly, not as fools but as wise" (Ephesians 5:15).

It's easy to have flawless conduct when the spotlight is glaring and people are watching. But what about our actions when no one is around? The great evangelist, Dwight L. Moody, said, "Character shows — even in the dark."

Be certain the word integrity is engraved on the cornerstone of your life.

Open your hearts to us. We have
wronged no one, we have corrupted
no one, we have cheated no one.
— 2 Corinthians 7:2

III.

PROMISES TO MYSELF

Promise #43

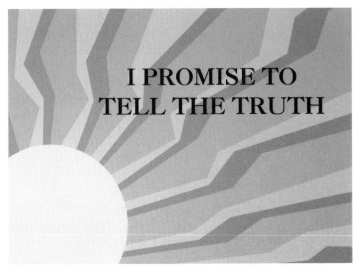

I PROMISE TO TELL THE TRUTH

W E HAVE BECOME a nation of liars. Deceit is such an ingrained part of our society that most people rarely stop to think about it. They pad their resumes, give phony excuses for their actions and constantly shade the truth.

We say, "How nice to see you," to people we can't stand. The phone rings, and we reply, "I'm sorry; she's not here right now," when the person is actually standing in the same room.

Experience tells us not to believe when we hear people say things such as, "The doctor will be with you shortly," "The check is in the mail" or "If I am elected."

The Wrong Answer

A minister in New Jersey announced, "Next week I'm preaching on deceit, and I want you to read Psalm 155."

The following Sunday, as he began his message, he asked, "How many have read the 155th Psalm?" Hands went up all across the sanctuary. "I don't want to disappoint you," he began, "but there is no 155th Psalm."

A recent *USA Today* poll revealed that only 56 percent of Americans teach honesty to their children. Are mothers and fathers so ashamed of their own behavior they avoid discussing the topic?

We can only wonder what the next generation of leaders will be like. A Louis Harris survey found that 65 percent of high school students surveyed admitted they would cheat on an important exam.

Crossing the Line

The title of "Fats" Waller's popular song is true:

"It's a Sin to Tell a Lie."

Let's stop kidding ourselves. When we willfully commit an act of deceit we break one of God's Ten Commandments: "You shall not bear false witness" (Exodus 20:16).

Make a declaration that, with the Lord's help, you will not cross the line between honesty and deception. God says, "I have no greater joy than to hear that my children walk in truth" (3 John 4). That is how the Almighty wants you to live.

Therefore, putting away lying,
"Let each one of you speak truth
with his neighbor," for we are
members of one another.
— Ephesians 4:25

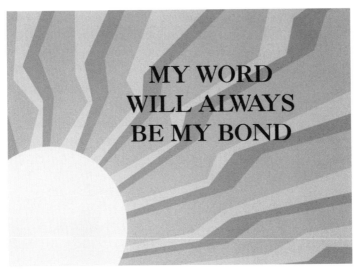

**MY WORD
WILL ALWAYS
BE MY BOND**

D O YOU SWEAR to tell the truth, the whole truth, and nothing but the truth, so help you God?" The witness is asked as he places his right hand on the Bible and answers, "I do."

As recent high-profile televised court cases have proved, taking an oath is just one more lie to the person whose heart is dishonest.

Haddon Robinson, in his book, *What Jesus Said About Successful Living,* says, "If we hire high-priced lawyers to build loopholes into our contracts, we are not truthful. When two people have a clear understanding between them, the contract shouldn't matter. When we give our word, that is all we have to give."

The courts agree. A verbal agreement is as legally binding as a written contract.

Yes and No

In Jesus' day, the Pharisees were experts on how to lie

by using oaths. They would use tricks such as swearing by the gold in the temple instead of the temple itself, or making an oath on the gift sitting on the altar instead of on the altar itself. The Lord mocked them, saying, "Fools and blind! For which is greater, the gift or the altar that sanctifies the gift?" (Matthew 23:19).

In His Sermon on the Mount, the Lord declared it was not necessary to take oaths at all. Instead, "Let your 'Yes' be 'Yes,' and your 'No,' 'No.' For whatever is more than these is from the evil one" (Matthew 5:37). What you say is much more than idle chatter.

Every word counts; it is part
of your permanent record.

The Trust Factor

Bill McCartney, former football coach at the University of Colorado and founder of the Promise Keepers men's movement, says, "If you want to take the [meaning of the] word *integrity* and reduce it to its simplest terms, you'd conclude that a man of integrity is a promise keeper. He's a guy who, when he says something, can be trusted. When he gives you his word, you can take it to the bank. His word is good."

Character is not a commodity that can be purchased. It is built by the decisions you permanently chisel on your heart. Strive for a reputation that will cause people to say, "He means what he says."

"For by your words you will be justified,
and by your words you will be condemned."
— Matthew 12:37

Promise #45

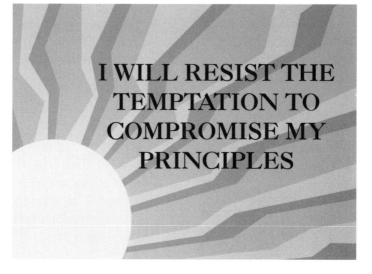

I WILL RESIST THE TEMPTATION TO COMPROMISE MY PRINCIPLES

WHERE DOES YOUR father work?" a schoolteacher asked a little girl in her class during a discussion on careers.

"I don't know," the first-grader replied, "but I guess he makes light bulbs and rolls of toilet paper because that's what he brings home in his lunch box."

We can listen to a thousand messages on the dangers of compromising our principles, but unless we make a personal decision, the words hold no meaning.

Jay Carty, in his book, *Something's Fishy,* talks about the advice he received from a friend when he started his ministry. The man warned him he should never take unreported cash for his personal use — even if it was only five dollars.

Carty explained, "He was telling me not to compromise a little, because a little almost always leads to a lot."

Jay was tested early in his ministry by the temptation to pocket cash received for the sale of his books and tapes at personal appearances. One month, when he was short of money, "I put sixty-four dollars in my wallet and used it to get home without entering it in the books. Over forty dollars remained burning in my britches five days later."

What happened? Jay recalls, "Was I going to compromise my ministry for sixty-four dollars? I couldn't stand it. I took out my checkbook, made up the difference and put that money back into the ministry."

Slow Decay

In a recent television interview, a Virginia prison official said, "Big-time thieves aren't born overnight. Our cells are brimming with people who began by stealing candy bars from the neighborhood grocery stores, and their appetites grew larger."

Like rust eats away at the foundation
of a bridge, our standards and principles
can slowly decay until one day the
entire structure collapses.

An accountant in Atlanta who was sentenced to prison for embezzling over six hundred thousand dollars from the bank where he worked, said, "It started with small sums. I'd pocket ten dollars and then twenty dollars and somehow justify it. Over time, it got out of hand until I was exposed."

Resist the slightest enticement to compromise your standards. You may be able to ignore the moral lapses of others, but you can never escape from you!

Therefore, brethren, stand fast and hold
the traditions which you were taught,
whether by word or our epistle.
— 2 Thessalonians 2:15

Promise #46

I PROMISE TO LISTEN MUCH MORE THAN I SPEAK

AFTER RETURNING FROM a trip to Russia, an article about my journey appeared in a local newspaper. The next day I received a phone call from an elderly woman who made an appointment to come to my office.

"Tell me about your trip," she asked as I helped her into the chair near my desk.

Then, almost before I could say a word, she began, "You know, I've been to Russia several times. My grandparents were born there before Stalin came to power."

She hadn't come to hear about my adventure. She had made the appointment in order to tell me about her's! So I enjoyed seeing how long I could keep her talking. I asked every question I could think of and politely listened.

After two hours the delightful woman glanced at her watch and announced, "Oh, my. I really must be going. But let me tell you something young man. You are one of the most interesting people I have ever talked with!"

A Powerful Key

In my experience, I know of no quicker way to make friends than to carefully listen to what someone is saying and to encourage the person to talk about their interests, not mine.

It takes restraint to remain quiet when your mind is flooded with dozens of thoughts, but the results are worth the effort. The writer of Proverbs states, "Even a fool is counted wise when he holds his peace; when he shuts his lips, he is considered perceptive" (Proverbs 17:28).

It's been said that knowledge
is power, and you don't gain that
power by talking but by listening.

There has never been a time in recorded history when so much information is instantly available. Thousands of books are on cassettes that can turn your automobile into a classroom on wheels. Most people, however, never take advantage of what is waiting at their fingertips. They would rather spend their time in idle conversation.

You can never become a storehouse of information when you are constantly disseminating information but never replenishing your supply. Make a conscious effort to listen much more than you speak. You will be amazed with the results.

"Take heed what you hear.
With the same measure you use,
it will be measured to you; and to
you who hear, more will be given."
— Mark 4:24

I WILL CONTROL MY THOUGHT LIFE

EVERY DAY, HUNDREDS — even *thousands* — of thoughts and ideas pass through our minds. Some are only fleeting notions that disappear as quickly as they arrive. Others become so dominant they effect not only our thinking but our emotions.

In his book, *As a Man Thinketh,* James Allen describes how this process affects our entire life. He says, "Into your hands will be placed the exact results of your own thoughts; you will receive that which you earn; no more, no less. Whatever your present environment may be, you will fall, remain or rise with your thoughts, your vision, your idea. You will become as small as your controlling desire; as great as your dominant aspiration." He goes on to say, "A man is literally what he thinks, his character being the complete sum of all his thoughts."

The apostle Paul taught the necessity of "bringing every thought into captivity to the obedience of Christ" (2 Corinthians 10:5).

Innovative Ideas

According to the noted writer, H. L. Mencken, "The average man never really thinks from end to end of his life. The mental activity of such people is only a mouthing of cliches. What they mistake for thought is simply repetition of what they have heard." Says Mencken, "My guess is that well over 80 percent of the human race goes through life without having one single original thought."

Ultimate Inspiration

What does God often do when He plans to move our world forward? He inspires a man or a woman with a brilliant new idea.

Just a quick glance at history shows the divine energy of a new thought. For example, Martin Luther grieved over the fact that people everywhere were trying to please God with their good works. Again and again, one phrase kept coming into his mind: "The just shall live by faith."

That one thought so consumed his spirit that he preached the message to anyone who would listen. As a result he launched the great Reformation which permanently changed the direction of the church.

What are the central thoughts of your life? What ideas are winning the battle for your attention? Guard them carefully because they will pull you toward themselves until your life will be a mirror image of those concepts.

For as he [a man] thinks
in his heart, so is he.
— Proverbs 23:7

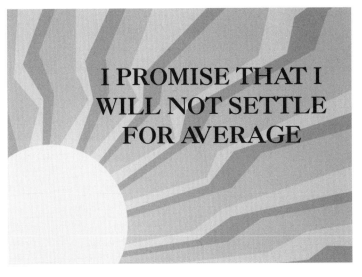

I PROMISE THAT I WILL NOT SETTLE FOR AVERAGE

IN MEMPHIS I once spoke with the owner of a restaurant who told me how difficult it was to find good help. He ran an ad for a cook and talked with two men and a woman about the job. At the end of each interview he asked this question: "If you get the job, how good do you think you can be at it?"

The first man answered, "I know I'll be good enough to get by."

The second responded, "I think I'm an average cook." The person he hired was the woman who told him, "Sir, I want to be the best cook you've ever had."

The owner smiled when he told me, "The greatest part of all is that she lived up to her desire."

Something Special

I've known scores of multi-talented people who have failed to make their mark in life by never breaking out of the norm. They are like the person described by writer

Elbert Hubbard, who observed, "As a rule, the man who can do all things equally well is a very mediocre individual."

Words like *normal, ordinary* and *typical* need to be eliminated from our vocabulary.

Bob Richards, the pole vaulter who won two Olympic gold medals, stated, "You don't win until you conquer the little flaws. You don't beat the great ones until your form is perfect. This is true in all of life. A flaw in a product can ruin a business. A personal failing, a little one, can ruin a person's life. Don't be content with mediocrity; strive to live up to the greatest within you."

The Warning

God warns of the danger of being average. He told the church in Laodicea, "I know your works, that you are neither cold nor hot. I could wish you were cold or hot. So then, because you are lukewarm, and neither cold nor hot, I will vomit you out of My mouth" (Revelation 3:15-16).

Don't be satisfied with a grade of fair or satisfactory. Instead, declare a personal war against mediocrity.

As John Mason said in his book, *An Enemy Called Average,* "Don't settle for an average life. God wants to launch you past the middle to the top."

"And whoever compels you to
go one mile, go with him two."
— Matthew 5:41

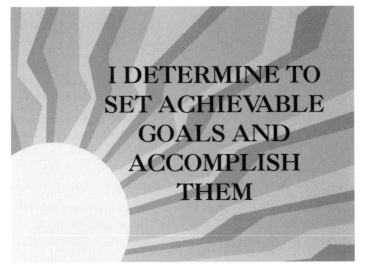

I DETERMINE TO SET ACHIEVABLE GOALS AND ACCOMPLISH THEM

UNTIL 1954, NOT one person on earth had run the mile in less than four minutes. It was as if a sign had been placed over that track and field event that said, "Impossible! It can't be done."

Roger Bannister, a physician and graduate of Oxford University, refused to accept what others thought impossible. That year on May 6, he astounded the world by running the mile in three minutes and 59.4 seconds.

Was the feat really that difficult? Evidently not. The next month his record was broken by Australian John Landy and since that time over twenty thousand people — including some school athletes — have accomplished the feat.

Why can so many do it now? Because in the mind of the athlete they no longer see the word *impossible*. Now, they see *achievable*.

The Small Tasks

Reaching your objective requires three important steps.

1. Believe the goal is possible.

2. Divide the task into a series of manageable steps.

3. Clearly write your plan.

Scripture tells us to "Write the vision and make it plain on tablets, that he may run who reads it" (Habakkuk 2:2).

Achieving your goal is rarely produced by a superhuman effort. Instead it is the result of faithfully doing many small but important tasks.

The captain of a large ship knows where he is headed — even if he can't see his next port of call for almost all of the journey. How does he arrive at his destination? By carefully plotting his charts and doing certain things in certain ways day after day.

You Have Help

Don't try to accomplish your goals alone. Realize God is your partner, and He will inspire you with a vision. He will also give you the ability to create a workable plan to accomplish your dream.

Never hesitate to enter the race. He will give you the strength it takes to complete the course and cross the finish line.

A man's heart plans his way,
but the Lord directs his steps.
— Proverbs 16:9

I WILL STAY FOCUSED ON MY OBJECTIVE

R ESPONDING TO A tip from an unhappy tax-payer, an investigative television reporter secretly filmed a day in the life of a repair crew for a utility company. What the reporter learned was shocking. Instead of working, the two repairmen visited three taverns and took a two-hour nap.

Majoring in Minors

The actions of those two men, unfortunately, are not unique. As popular author Denis Waitley observes, "People waste most of their waking hours every day going through the motions, chatting idly, shuffling paper, putting off decisions, reacting, majoring in minors and concentrating on trivia. They spend their time in low priority tension relieving, rather than high priority goal-achieving activities."

What good are written goals if you randomly chase any object that captures your attention? There's an African proverb that says, "He who hunts two rats, catches none."

The apostle Paul didn't wait to see which way the wind was blowing before deciding on a course of action. He declared, "Brethren, I do not count myself to have apprehended; but one thing I do, forgetting those things which are behind and reaching forward to those things which are ahead, I press toward the goal for the prize of the upward call of God in Christ Jesus" (Philippians 3:13-14).

An Eye Exam

Don't overlook the details. Giant corporations don't suddenly skyrocket to the top by chance. They have a business plan they adhere to meticulously. Their "bean counters" can give you a current financial and sales report on any given day.

We need to conduct our personal life with the same attention to detail. How long has it been since you have taken an inventory? Would you be embarrassed if someone asked to see the way your files are organized and your financial records kept?

God told the people in King Solomon's day to "Be diligent to know the state of your flocks, and attend to your herds" (Proverbs 27:23). Stay alert. Make a promise to keep your eyes focused on the prize.

May He grant you according to your
heart's desire, and fulfill all your purpose
— Psalm 20:4

I COMMIT
TO ACCEPT
CHALLENGES
THAT WILL HELP
ME GROW

IN OUR DYNAMIC world, nothing remains static. Flowers bloom and fade, oceans rise and fall, and the earth is shaken by earthquakes and volcanoes.

You are also in a constant state of transformation. Charles Garfield, author of *Peak Performance,* says you need to "recognize yourself as a person who was born not as a peak performer but as a learner, with the capacity to grow, change, and reach for the highest possibilities of human nature."

Each of us could wear a T-shirt with the slogan "Work in Progress!"

Daily, we need to ask, "What more can I be? What else can I achieve that will benefit me and my associates? What can I do that will contribute to my family, my community and my church?"

Is It Over?

When you're confronted with a giant obstacle it's easy

to throw your hands up and cry, "It's over. My best days are behind me!"

Wrong. It can mark the inauguration of a great new beginning. Don't be afraid to face tough times.

A real leader has been described as
being like a teabag — not worth much
until he's been through some hot water.

A Dose of Adversity

Psychologist James Dobson, in his book, *When God Doesn't Make Sense,* discusses the "adversity principle" at work in the world. "As strange as it seems," he says, "habitual well-being is not advantageous to a species."

As an example, Dobson talks about a tree planted in a rain forest. "Because water is readily available it does not have to extend its root system more than a few inches below the surface. Consequently, it is often poorly anchored and can be toppled by a minor windstorm. But a mesquite tree planted in a hostile and arid land must send its roots down thirty feet or more in search of water. Not even a gale can blow it over."

Welcome every challenge as a necessary force to strengthen your character and drive your foundation deeper.

Consider it pure joy, my brothers,
whenever you face trials of many kinds,
because you know that testing of your faith
develops perseverance. Perseverance must
finish its work so that you may be mature
and complete, not lacking anything.
— James 1:2-4, NIV

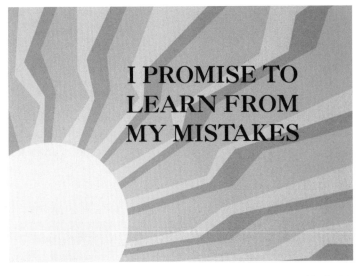

I PROMISE TO LEARN FROM MY MISTAKES

TOM WATSON, FOUNDER of IBM recalled the time one of his young vice presidents took the initiative on the development of a new product. It was an extremely risky venture that became a colossal failure and cost the company ten million dollars.

Watson called the executive to his office and said, "There's a matter we need to discuss."

Convinced he was on the verge of being fired, the young executive blurted out, "I guess you want my resignation?"

"You must be kidding," Watson replied. "We've just spent ten million dollars educating you!"

Mistakes are not the end of the world. In many ways they are the beginning of knowledge.

Food for Growth

How important are your errors? Rick Patino, coach of the University of Kentucky Wildcats, says, "Failure is good. It's fertilizer. Everything I have learned about coaching, I've learned from making mistakes."

Far too often we treat a minor error as if it's a permanent condition. There is a huge difference. In the words of a Portuguese proverb:

"Stumbling is not falling."

Ronald Reagan was a master at putting his errors in the past. Said the former president, "Now what should happen when you make a mistake is this: You take your knocks, you learn your lessons and then you move on. That's the healthiest way to deal with a problem."

Saul's Admission

The Old Testament records the rocky relationship between King Saul and David. When Saul was pursuing David, David had an opportunity to kill him while Saul and his army slept in their camp. David's nephew, Abishai, had gone down into the camp with David and was going to spear Saul to kill him. But David had compassion on Saul and said, "Do not destroy him; for who can stretch out his hand against the Lord's anointed, and be guiltless?" (1 Samuel 26:9).

It was not long until Saul confessed, "I have sinned. Return, my son David. For I will harm you no more, because my life was precious in your eyes this day. Indeed I have played the fool and erred exceedingly" (v. 21). Like Saul, we can learn from our mistakes.

The Lord upholds all who fall, and
raises up all who are bowed down.
— Psalm 145:14

Promise #53

I WILL SAY I'M WRONG WHEN I REALLY AM

DIDN'T YOU JUST miss the road to Columbus?" I asked a friend who was driving me back to the campus of Ohio State University when I was a student there.

"Don't you think I know where I'm going?" he abruptly snapped back. I opened the glove compartment and took out the map and tried to tell him we were headed miles out of our way, but he wouldn't listen.

"No problem. We'll get there," he tried to reassure me.

My fellow student could never bring himself to admit his error in navigation — even when we arrived at the campus nearly two hours late.

Shifting the Blame

For many people, the three most difficult words to say are these: "I was wrong." They will invent excuses, deflect blame or simply remain silent to avoid confessing they are at fault.

We know that confession is good for the soul, but it's certainly tough on the ego.

English author and clergyman Jonathan Swift wrote, "A man should never be ashamed to own he has been in the wrong, which is but saying, in other words, that he is wiser today than he was yesterday."

Lessons From the Hog Farm

Do you remember the story of the prodigal son? He took his inheritance and went to a foreign country where he squandered everything in wild living.

A great famine came to the land, and he took a job feeding pigs, hoping to eat some of the leftovers. There, in that lowly pig pen, he came to his senses and admitted that leaving home had been a huge mistake. He knew his father's servants had food to spare, yet his stomach was growling.

The young man said, "I will arise and go to my father, and will say to him, 'Father, I have sinned against heaven and before you'" (Luke 15:18).

You know how the story ends. His father welcomed him with open arms and gave him a royal welcome fit for a king.

Never become too proud to admit your errors. Confession brings a freedom and liberation that is both necessary and refreshing.

He who covers his sins will not
prosper, but whoever confesses
and forsakes them will have mercy.
— Proverbs 28:13

I AFFIRM TO DEVELOP MY TALENTS TO THEIR MAXIMUM POTENTIAL

MARK TWAIN ONCE told a story about a man who died and met Saint Peter at the pearly gates. Realizing Saint Peter was a wise and knowledgeable person, he said, "Saint Peter, I have been interested in military history for many years. Tell me who was the greatest general of all times?"

Saint Peter quickly responded, "Oh, that's a simple question. It is that man right over there," as he pointed nearby.

The man said, "You must be mistaken, Saint Peter. I knew that man on earth. He was just a common laborer."

"That's right, my friend," replied Saint Peter. "But he would have been the greatest general of all time — if he had been a general."

Declare Your Intentions

God creates each of us with natural abilities and guides us toward a particular focus for our life. That's only the starting point; the next step is ours. We have an obligation to expand that potential to its ultimate destiny.

Discover what you are supposed to do and do it! Michelangelo said:

> *"It is only well with me when*
> *I have a chisel in my hand."*

Lawrence O. Kitchen made it to the top of the huge Lockheed Corporation despite the fact that he never received a college degree. How did he accomplish that feat? By enrolling in dozens of adult education courses — from night classes at a local community college to corporate-sponsored training seminars. By the time he reached mid-management people didn't care whether or not he had the credentials. Kitchen could do the job.

Your Supply

Recognize the source of your gift. Peter declared, "If anyone speaks, let him speak as the oracles of God. If anyone ministers, let him do it as with the ability which God supplies, that in all things God may be glorified" (1 Peter 4:11). What will you do today to develop the unique talent the Lord has given to you?

> *Most assuredly, I say to you, he who*
> *believes in Me, the works that I do he will*
> *do also; and greater works than these he*
> *will do, because I go to My Father.*
> *— John 14:12*

I WILL ELIMINATE UNHEALTHY FEAR AND WORRY

W HAT ARE YOU afraid of?" asked the *Times* of London in a survey on fear. The results were surprising.

I thought the number one anxiety would be the fear of dying, but that was number seven with only 19 percent. Ranked six through two were the fear of illness (19 percent), the fear of deep water (22 percent), the fear of financial disaster (22 percent), the fear of insects and spiders (22 percent) and the fear of heights (32 percent).

What did people dread the most? It was the fear of public speaking (41 percent). Fortunately, this is an anxiety we can greatly reduce with practice and experience.

A Ring of Fire

It's human nature to fear the unknown. For example, in the Middle Ages, European sailors refused to sail very far south because they were convinced the earth was ringed with fire. They knew the farther south they traveled, the hotter the temperature would be. A painting from that era depicted a ship turning back into the Mediterranean Sea with the Latin phrase, *ne plus ultra,* meaning "nothing more beyond." It took men like Ponce de Leon and Christopher Columbus to challenge that myth. Learn to recognize the difference between healthy and unhealthy fear.

> *Reality-based concern founded on fact is vital because it prepares us for potential danger. Imagined fear, however, damages our emotional well-being.*

Answers for Anxiety

Today, millions of people suffer from harmful worry. Psychologists have identified an extensive list of phobias from claustrophobia — the morbid terror of confined places — to monophobia — the dread of being alone.

One of the most frequently used phrases in the Bible is "Fear not." Those were God's words to Jacob, Joshua, Joseph and many others. "For I, the Lord your God, will hold your right hand, saying to you, 'Fear not, I will help you'" (Isaiah 41:13).

Through prayer, positive self-talk, and focusing on behavior, not feelings, we can conquer unhealthy anxiety. We also need to exchange fear for love since the Word tells us that "perfect love casts out fear" (1 John 4:18). There is no need to struggle with the burden of crippling fright when help is available.

> *"Be strong and of good courage; do not be afraid, nor be dismayed, for the Lord your God is with you wherever you go."*
> *— Joshua 1:9*

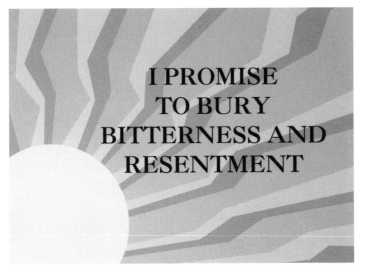

I PROMISE TO BURY BITTERNESS AND RESENTMENT

C AN YOU IMAGINE what would happen if you tried to put one hundred pounds of air pressure in a tire that was designed to hold thirty-five pounds? There would be an explosion.

That's what happens to people who have no safety valve to release the tension of their bitterness and resentment.

I have met people whose hostility knows no boundaries. They are indignant with themselves, with those around them and with the world in general. They brood over a perceived offense day after day until it begins to burn like acid on their heart and soul. They act out the definition of the word *resentment,* which means "to feel again."

The Physical Reality

Medical research has found that extended bitterness can have a profound impact on health. If unchecked, these deep feelings lead to an extreme emotional state. The strain and stress take a physical toll and result in a distressing illness.

Internal strife has been found to reduce natural antibodies and increase our susceptibility to infection. It's also linked to heart attacks, strokes, weight loss or gain and can lead to clinical depression. As the writer of Proverbs states:

A sound heart is life to the body,
but envy is rottenness to the bones.
— Proverbs 14:30

Resentment is usually a one-way street, and we are the ones who are harmed. The person with whom we hold the grudge may not even be aware of our feelings.

Learning the Lesson

A forced smile will never hide what is smoldering inside. The truth will make its way to the surface. Scripture tells us that "Where envy and self-seeking exist, confusion and every evil thing are there" (James 3:16).

God can forgive and forget, but we have great difficulty with that process. Ask forgiveness for your past and value what you've learned from the experience. You can keep your commitment, with the Lord's help, to rise above hostility, indignation and strife.

Do not speak evil of one another, brethren.
He who speaks evil of a brother and judges
his brother, speaks evil of the law and
judges the law. But if you judge the law,
you are not a doer of the law but a judge.
— James 4:11

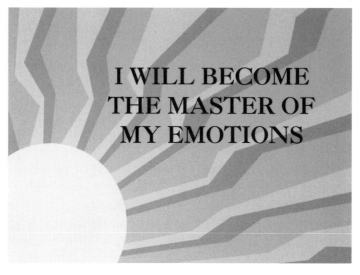

I WILL BECOME THE MASTER OF MY EMOTIONS

A DVERTISING COPYWRITERS ON Madison Avenue learned long ago that people don't always buy because of quality and price. We respond when our passions and feelings are touched. We buy the sizzle, not the steak.

Here are sales pitches from recent magazine ads:

Outrageously delicious.
Revel in the unexpected.
Don't simply imagine it. Indulge in it!

In earlier days, people would ask, "What do you think about it?" Now they ask, "How do you feel about it?"

Being guided by emotions, however, is not a new phenomenon. God created us as body, soul and spirit — capable of joy, happiness, fear, guilt and grief. When Joseph saw his brothers in Egypt he "made haste and sought somewhere to weep. And he went into his chamber and wept there" (Genesis 43:30). The shortest verse in the

Bible is one of the most revealing: "Jesus wept" (John 11:35).

According to Billy Graham, "There are many dangers of false emotionalism, but that does not rule out true emotion and depth of feeling. Emotion may vary in religious experience. Some people are stoical and others are demonstrative, but the feeling will be there. There is going to be a tug at the heart."

Taking Charge

How do we respond in a highly-charged dangerous situation? In most cases we are guided by a basic "fight or flight" principle we inherited from our ancestors — we either battle or run. Often, however, our choices are more complex. We can use psychology, logic or other means of persuasion to resolve the issue.

Becoming master of your emotions doesn't mean you have to deny your feelings or become cold and calculating. Instead, become totally aware of what is taking place inside and let your heart lead the way without allowing yourself to be governed by instant knee-jerk reactions.

God created us to have dominion over the earth and over ourselves. We can meet His expectation by living a well-balanced life.

*There is therefore now no
condemnation to those who are in Christ
Jesus, who do not walk according to the
flesh, but according to the Spirit.
— Romans 8:1*

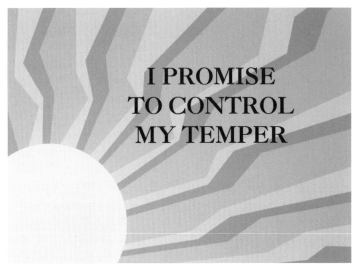

I PROMISE TO CONTROL MY TEMPER

RECENTLY, AT A men's retreat in Ohio, I presented a seminar with the double-edge title, "How to Lose Our Temper." After the session, a man spoke with me privately concerning his life-long battle with rage that was often out of control.

"It has caused great personal harm," he confessed, "that has affected my family and my business." That night he made a promise to himself and to God to take authority over his temper. It was an important first step.

Anger is an emotion that is mentioned hundreds of times in Scripture and not always in a negative light. The Bible talks about God's wrath and how it's used to correct His people.

Redirect Your Energy

We are told to "Be angry, and do not sin" (Ephesians 4:26). How is that possible? Our fury, if directed properly, can produce positive results.

Gary Oliver, a Christian counselor from Colorado, gives two examples: "Abraham Lincoln invested the energy of his anger at the brutality of slavery to make changes in the country's laws and emancipate the slaves and abolish slavery. Ghandi invested the energy of his anger at the plight of his people and the nation of India was born."

Have you ever noticed how a flashbulb can temporarily blind you when someone takes your picture? Anger affects us in much the same way. For a moment, it can cause our logical and rational abilities to vanish. Fortunately, our anger rarely lasts long. That's why it's important to delay our reaction.

Thomas Jefferson once said, "When angry, count to ten before you speak; if very angry, count to a hundred."

Under Control

If you are not careful, your outrage can be like a snow-ball rolling downhill. It can become a force you can't control and the results could spell disaster. The Word tells us, "A quick-tempered man acts foolishly, and a man of wicked intentions is hated" (Proverbs 14:17). Take charge of your temper.

He who is slow to anger is better
than the mighty, and he who rules his
spirit [better] than he who takes a city.
— Proverbs 16:32

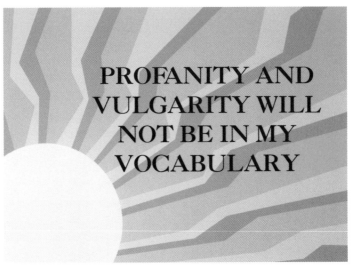

PROFANITY AND VULGARITY WILL NOT BE IN MY VOCABULARY

A MAN WHO worked at a factory was known by his friends to have a foul mouth. If the slightest thing went wrong he would fill the air with cursing. When this man was fifty-two years old, a co-worker invited him to visit his church where the man had a profound spiritual conversion.

Two weeks later, when the minister gave an opportunity for people to give a short testimony, the man stood and said, "As you know, I recently gave my heart to the Lord in this church. I asked God to not only cleanse my heart but also my mouth. I wanted Him to take away my profanity."

He continued, "On Saturday morning I had my first real test. I slammed the car door on my thumb, and do you know what I said?"

The congregation fell silent waiting for his reply.

"I shouted, 'Oh, sugar!' And that's when I knew I was truly changed."

Recently I visited a home and heard a small child use a curse word she obviously didn't understand. "Oh, she says the most surprising things," her mother exclaimed without the slightest reprimand.

I couldn't help but wonder what the girl's vocabulary would be when she reached her teenage years.

Time for Restraint

Those whose words are constantly laced with vulgarity not only destroy their reputation but are an offense to their Creator. We need to heed the words of the psalmist:

> *I will guard my ways, lest I sin with my*
> *tongue; I will restrain my mouth with a*
> *muzzle, while the wicked are before me.*
> *— Psalm 39:1*

Profanity is more than bad taste; it is a sign of a poor vocabulary. To some people, a curse word becomes a substitute for saying *uh* or *um* — and often is such a habitual response that the person no longer hears the words.

When a man in Virginia was asked to stop using the word "Christ" in a negative way, he responded, "I don't say that, do I?" It was only when the man's conversation was tape recorded that he finally recognized the depth of the problem. If you must swear, swear that your words will not be profane but pure.

> *He who has a deceitful heart*
> *finds no good, and he who has*
> *a perverse tongue falls into evil.*
> *— Proverbs 17:20*

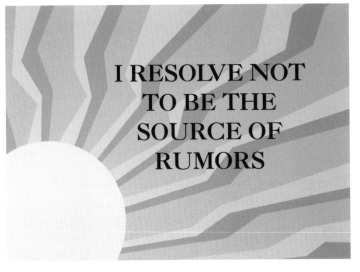

I RESOLVE NOT TO BE THE SOURCE OF RUMORS

A WOMAN WHO had worked as a bank teller for fourteen years couldn't understand why her fellow employees were suddenly shunning her. They avoided her at coffee breaks and no longer invited her to join them at lunch.

"Do you really think she did it?" her co-workers whispered to each other.

A few days later, the president of the bank called her to his office and said, "Several thousand dollars of cash cannot be accounted for, and we believe you are responsible."

"That's preposterous!" she replied. "I would never do anything like that."

She was placed on an immediate leave of absence and rumors, greatly embellishing the accusation, began to circulate in the community, in her church and even at the school her children attended.

Four months later, when federal bank examiners finished their investigation, the chief accountant for the bank was arrested for fraud and was proven guilty in a public trial.

What happened to this lady? The false accusation had so deeply affected her life and her family that they decided to move to another community and start over.

Napoleon said:

> *"There are different ways of assassinating a man — by pistol, sword, poison, or moral assassination. They are the same in their results except that the last is more cruel."*

The Danger of Hearsay

Our system of justice is based on the premise that we are innocent until proven guilty. In reality, however, the process is reversed. One small rumor can ruin a person's reputation for life.

Gossip has been called a "little sin," but it can cause havoc — disrupting families, dividing communities and destroying churches.

What God told the children of Israel is still true today: "You shall not go about as a talebearer among your people; nor shall you take a stand against the life of your neighbor: I am the Lord" (Leviticus 19:16). Resolve not to spread unfounded rumors. There's too much at stake.

> *He who covers a transgression*
> *seeks love, but he who repeats*
> *a matter separates friends.*
> *— Proverbs 17:9*

Promise #61

I PROMISE TO DEFEAT MY NEGATIVE HABITS

WHAT CROSSES YOUR mind when you think about harmful behavior? Do you reflect on people who are trapped by a psychological and chemical dependence on alcohol, drugs or tobacco? Do you think about those who struggle with anorexia or bulimia? Or the person who battles compulsive gambling?

The media has focused our attention on only a handful of sins that plague our society. Sadly, the list looms much longer. I have met people who are addicted to computer games, perfectionism, religious legalism — even country music. Any activity that has a controlling vice-grip on your life needs to be examined carefully.

The Breakdown

The consequences of a negative habit can be enormous — the loss of a job, a fatal accident or a serious health problem. Our lives can literally fall apart without self-control. The Word tells us, "Whoever has no rule over his own spirit is like a city broken down, without walls" (Proverbs 25:28).

Recovery programs such as the Twelve Steps established by Alcoholics Anonymous have helped millions escape their addiction to alcoholism. The same principles have aided those trapped by compulsive overeating, compulsive shopping, sex addiction and other obsessions and habits.

Can spiritual renewal change our behavior? History shows that it can. The awakening that swept England at the turn of the century was remarkable. Eifion Evans, in his book, *The Welsh Revival of 1904,* said, "Convictions for drunkenness in Glamorgan [county] fell from 10,528 in 1903 to 5,490 in 1906." It was claimed that "three months of the revival had done more to sober the county than the temperance effort of many years."

Time for Recovery

In a nutshell, here are six declarations that hold the key to eliminating a negative habit.

1. I admit I have a problem.

2. I realize there is a higher power that will help me.

3. I am willing to change.

4. I am willing to mend my broken relationships.

5. I will monitor my progress.

6. I will seek God's continuing help.

He who has begun a good work
in you will complete it until the
day of Jesus Christ.
— Philippians 1:6

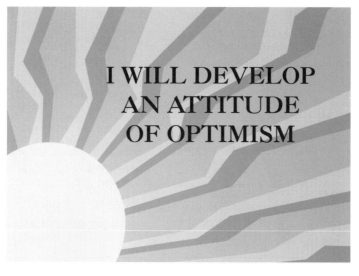

I WILL DEVELOP
AN ATTITUDE
OF OPTIMISM

F OR YEARS, A man in Oklahoma City was dominated by the weather. If it was overcast and raining
he was depressed, but if the sun was shining and the
sky was blue, he was on top of the world.

Finally, he made the decision to take charge of his attitude.
He learned to get up in the morning, look out the window
and, whether it was raining or radiant, would say, "This is
exactly what kind of day I ordered!"

What Is Our Vision?

A pessimist has been defined as "someone who feels
bad when he feels good for fear he'll feel worse later."

Perhaps you can name five or ten people right now who
are specialists in gloom and doom. If a golden opportunity
were handed to them on a silver platter they would tell you
that the gold will fade and the silver will tarnish. Can such
a person change? Can the wrinkles be erased from their
brow?

Don't believe those who tell you, "Some people are born to see the glass half full, and others are born to see the glass half empty." It's not true.

> *We were born with a spirit of wonder and optimism that remains unless we allow it to be destroyed by outside forces.*

It Is a Choice

Negative expectation greatly limits your potential. As John Maxwell, whose leadership seminars have made a positive impact on thousands, states, "When we become conditioned to perceived truth and closed to new possibilities, the following happens: we see what we *expect* to see, not what we *can* see. We hear what we *expect* to hear, not what we *can* hear. We think what we *expect* to think, not what we *can* think."

Jesus gave the ultimate message of faith, hope and belief when He declared, "Therefore I say to you, whatever things you ask when you pray, believe that you receive them, and you will have them" (Mark 11:24).

Optimism is a choice. Every day you decide what the hours will hold. From your heart, declare, "This is the day the Lord has made! I will rejoice and be glad in it."

> *Finally, brethren, whatever things are true, whatever things are noble, whatever things are just, whatever things are pure, whatever things are lovely, whatever things are of good report, if there is any virtue and if there is anything praiseworthy; meditate on these things.*
> *— Philippians 4:8*

Promise #63

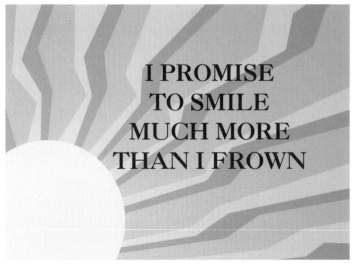

I PROMISE TO SMILE MUCH MORE THAN I FROWN

I N KANSAS CITY, many people still talk about Vick Pearce, who drove a city bus for over thirty years. Riders called it the "happy bus."

His passengers laughed, shared books and recipes — and even exchanged Christmas cookies. It had nothing to do with the bus but everything to do with the driver. Until the day he retired, Vick greeted every passenger with a big grin, a hearty "Good Morning," and encouraged even the shyest person to enter in. Said Pearce, "The way I liked to be treated is the way I treated them."

Breaking Barriers

I've been asked, "Neil, why do you smile so much?"

I jokingly told one fellow, "Well, God gave me a short upper lip." But the real reason I smile is because I'm happy — it's just that simple. Plus, I realized long ago that when I smile, people return the favor.

In my travels, especially in countries where English isn't

spoken, a pleasant countenance is worth a thousand words. Once, in West Africa, a group of young men became extremely agitated when I started taking photos in their village. They approached me with menacing glares, speaking a language I didn't understand. Rather than running away, I immediately put my camera down, sat on the steps of a village store and flashed them my biggest smile. I then pulled out a set of pictures I recently had developed and showed them what I was doing. They not only enjoyed the photos but started grinning and pointing to their own faces as if to say, "Will you take my picture, too?" Of course, I did.

Concert performer Victor Borge observes:

"A smile is the shortest
distance between two people."

Display Your Delight

The Lord showed how He wants us to live when He spoke through the prophet Isaiah. He said, "For you shall go out with joy, and be led out with peace; the mountains and the hills shall break forth into singing before you, and all the trees of the field shall clap their hands" (Isaiah 55:12).

Since it takes twenty-six muscles to smile and sixty-two to frown, why not make it easy on yourself? Relax — start smiling.

A merry heart makes a cheerful
countenance, but by sorrow of
the heart the spirit is broken.
— Proverbs 15:13

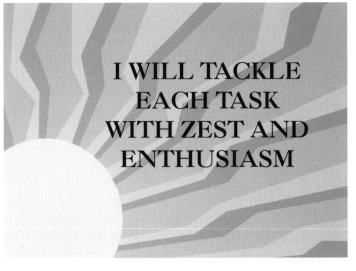

I WILL TACKLE EACH TASK WITH ZEST AND ENTHUSIASM

A T A BUSY construction site, an eight-year-old boy walked up to the contractor who was surveying a tall office tower he was building. "Tell me, mister," the young fellow said, "how can I be important like you when I grow up?"

The gray-haired man smiled and answered, "It's easy, son. Buy a red shirt and work like crazy!"

Then the wealthy builder of the skyscraper pointed up into the framework of the new structure. "Do you see all those men up there?"

"Yes," the boy replied, squinting as he looked up.

"See that man in the red shirt?" the contractor continued. "I don't even know his name, but I've been watching how hard he works. One of these days I'm going to need a new superintendent, and I'll go to that fellow and say, 'Hey, you in the red shirt, come here!' He's the one who will get the chance."

If we seize each opportunity with enthusiasm, someone will surely notice.

Publisher Malcolm Forbes observed, "Men who never get carried away should be." He added, "If you're kicking and screaming about reaching or not reaching a goal, at least we know you're alive."

Don't be afraid to add fire to your faith —
even if some may call you a fanatic.

A Tiny Difference

The "little extra" that is the automatic byproduct of enthusiasm marks the distinction between average and excellence.

Often, the small difference can be profound. For example, a race car that runs just a few seconds faster than its competitors can double its value. In the Olympics, the score of a gold medal gymnast may be only a fraction of a point higher than second place.

Add passion and exuberance to everything you do — at home, at work or at church. The apostle Paul wrote to the Christians at Corinth, "Since you are zealous for spiritual gifts, let it be for the edification of the church that you seek to excel" (1 Corinthians 14:12).

God's world is dynamic, vibrant and exciting. Be sure your life reflects it.

But it is good to be zealous in a
good thing always, and not only
when I am present with you.
— Galatians 4:18

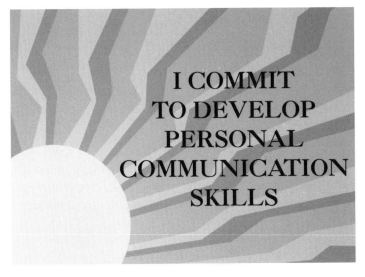

I COMMIT TO DEVELOP PERSONAL COMMUNICATION SKILLS

SINCE YOU HAVE a message worth sharing, why not sharpen your verbal skills? We always mean to say the right thing, but sometimes the message can be misinterpreted.

- The sponsor of one of my seminars wrote, "I cannot recommend this gentleman too highly."

- Just before speaking to a rotary club, the program chairman turned and said, "Shall we let them enjoy themselves a little longer, or shall we have your speech now?"

- A reader wrote, "Thanks for sending me a copy of your book. I'll waste no time reading it."

One, Two, Three

Here are three rules for improving your speech:

1. Use simple, clear words.

The National Council of Teachers of English gives an annual "Doublespeak" award. The Pentagon called combat "violence processing" and peace "permanent pre-hostility."

2. Speak directly to the point.

Lincoln used 267 words for the Gettysburg Address. The Lord's prayer contains only sixty-six. Yet a U.S. government order dealing with the price of oranges contained a whopping 28,561 words!

3. Keep your communication personal.

A salesman phoned a client and a secretary glibly answered, "211-8412."

"May I speak to Mr. Taylor?" asked, the man, slightly irritated.

"Can I tell him who's calling?" replied the secretary.

"819-3595," was the salesman's tongue-in-cheek response.

It's never too late to take a short course in interpersonal skills, public speaking or vocabulary building.

And my speech and my preaching
were not with persuasive words
of human wisdom, but in demonstration
of the Spirit and of power.
— 1 Corinthians 2:4

I PROMISE TO DEMONSTRATE GOOD MANNERS

WHEN WE SHAKE hands it's a natural friendly gesture. However, the custom originated in the Middle Ages. When two men met they extended their right arms and shook hands to show they did not intend to use their swords. It was a display of courtesy and goodwill.

The practice of good manners started even earlier. In the book of Genesis, when two angels came to the entrance of the city of Sodom, Lot "rose up to meet them, and he bowed himself" (Genesis 19:1).

For many, being polite has become a lost art. Someone once commented, "I don't recall your name, but your manners are familiar."

A Matter of Respect

Etiquette is not limited to knowing how to make a proper introduction or learning which knife or fork to use at a formal banquet. Courtesies reflect your basic values of honesty, fairness, caring, accountability and even promise keeping.

Charles and Anne Winters, who head a national etiquette training program say, "Practicing good manners is how we treat others with honor, dignity and respect."

There are hundreds of rules for proper behavior, but almost all of them are based on your response to this question: Do I think of others more than myself?

Let's look at an example. If you write a thank you note to your hostess for dinner, which of these two phrases is likely to generate a return invitation? "I had a wonderful time!" or "You are a wonderful hostess!" I don't have to tell you the answer.

Little Keys

Many adults need to memorize this poem taught to a first grade class:

> *Hearts, like doors, will open*
> *with ease, to very, very little keys.*
> *And don't forget that two of these are,*
> *"I thank you" and "If you please."*

What about you? Do you still open a door for a total stranger and let others enter or exit an elevator first? Remember: You never get a second chance to make a first impression.

> *Let no one despise your youth, but be an*
> *example to the believers in word, in conduct,*
> *in love, in spirit, in faith, in purity.*
> *— 1 Timothy 4:12*

I WILL EFFICIENTLY MANAGE MY TIME

A N EMPLOYMENT OFFICER inquired of a job applicant, "Why did you leave your previous job?" The applicant replied, "They insisted that all employees get to work by 8:45 every morning, and I could not work under those stringent conditions."

Needless to say, he wasn't hired.

For many, the clock presents a great challenge. A junior executive with a food distribution company was a whiz at writing marketing plans and had great rapport with his staff. Yet he was constantly passed over for promotions because he lacked the ability to manage his time. "His phone calls are at least four times longer than the average employee," his boss complained.

A Hole in Your Bucket

How are valuable moments squandered? Paul J. Meyer, founder of Success Motivation Institute, states, "Most time is wasted, not in hours, but in minutes. A bucket with a small hole in the bottom gets just as empty as a bucket that is deliberately kicked over."

We live in a world of great contrasts. However, in one area we are all on equal footing. The legendary Texas retailer, Stanley Marcus, was once asked what the super-successful people he knew had in common. "They all have twenty-four-hour days," he observed. "The world has expanded in almost all directions, but everyone receives the same ration of hours each day. The difference is how you use them."

The apostle Paul advised the believers at Ephesus:

*See then that you walk circumspectly, not
as fools but as wise, redeeming the time.*
— Ephesians 5:15-16

Keeping Pace

To understand the value of a minute, take a tip from your accountant or attorney. The moment you phone for advice, expect him to make an entry on his time log and add the prorated charge to your bill.

There's a lesson we can learn from a clerk in a Denver department store. He said, "I used to waste time watching the clock. Then one day it dawned on me that the hands of the clock kept moving at a steady pace. I figured if I was going to keep up, I'd better start moving, too!"

Instead of counting minutes, make your minutes count.

*To everything there is a season, a
time for every purpose under heaven.*
— Ecclesiastes 3:1

I PLEDGE TO ELIMINATE PROCRASTINATION

IN NORTH DAKOTA I heard about a flock of geese heading south to escape the coming winter. They landed in a farmer's field and filled themselves with corn. The next morning as the sun was coming up, they flew on. However, one goose stayed behind. "This corn is delicious," he said. "I think I'll stay one more day. There might not be any food where my friends are headed."

The next morning and the day after that, he decided to delay again. The pattern continued, and he kept saying, "Tomorrow I will fly south."

Before long the winter winds became so turbulent that waiting any longer would mean certain death for the goose. He lifted his wings, waddled across the field and tried to pick up enough speed to soar into the air. Sadly, he had waited too long. He was too fat to fly!

A Five Step Plan

The difference between an achiever and an "also-ran" is

self-discipline. Writer John Erskine observed, "In the simplest terms, a leader is one who knows where he wants to go, then gets up and goes."

How can you break the chains of procrastination? Here are five helpful steps:

1. *Adopt a short-term strategy.* Ask yourself, What can I do in the next five minutes?

2. *Use the do-it-yourself approach.* Don't wait for help. As Charles De Gaulle said, "Deliberation is the work of many men. Action, of only one alone."

3. *Schedule the task you dread.* Write it on your calendar as something you absolutely, positively will do no matter what!

4. *Don't worry about mistakes.* Immediate action is more important than a flawless performance.

5. *Stop thinking and start doing.* When Alexander the Great was asked how he conquered the world, he replied, "By not delaying."

Think about what hurdles you need to overcome, then take the first leap.

> *Do not say to your neighbor, "Go*
> *and come back, and tomorrow I will*
> *give it," when you have it with you.*
> *— Proverbs 3:28*

I WILL STOP MAKING EXCUSES

I WAS INVITED to present a seminar at the Memorial Center in Washington Crossing, Pennsylvania. Across the front of the auditorium was a large mural of George Washington crossing the nearly-frozen Delaware River in a small boat on Christmas day, 1776.

The painting depicted the dramatic story of a man who had plenty of excuses to turn back. It was bitterly cold. He had to break through the ice. The enemy was waiting on the other side — plus it was Christmas.

Washington, however, ignored the obstacles. This was the Revolutionary War, and he was determined to defend the Declaration of Independence. The next day, his army won a great victory at Trenton.

Broken Strings

When things go haywire, it's not the time for an alibi. It's time for an accomplishment.

The gifted violinist Paganini was playing a concert

when one of the strings popped and hung down the violin. As he continued playing, a second string broke, then the third.

Rather than stop the concert, Paganini held up his violin and announced, "One string and Paganini!" He placed the instrument under his chin and began playing a song so magnificent the audience gave him a standing ovation. The violinist made no excuses. He did the best with what he had.

Replaced at the Table

Jesus told the parable of the man who prepared a great banquet, only the invited guests were no-shows. "They all with one accord began to make excuses. The first said to him, 'I have bought a piece of ground, and I must go and see it. I ask you to have me excused.' And another said, 'I have bought five yoke of oxen, and I am going to test them. I ask you to have me excused.' Still another said, 'I have married a wife, and therefore I cannot come'" (Luke 14:18-20).

Their places at the table were taken by the poor, the crippled, the blind and the lame. Even more, those who originally refused the invitation would never have the chance to eat at the table again.

Receive the bounty God has prepared. Eliminate your excuses.

Then the man said, "The woman whom
You gave to be with me, she gave me
of the tree, and I ate." And the Lord
God said to the woman, "What is this
you have done?" And the woman said,
"The serpent deceived me, and I ate."
— Genesis 3:12-13

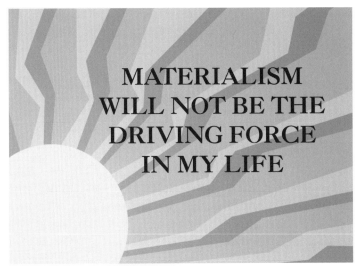

MATERIALISM WILL NOT BE THE DRIVING FORCE IN MY LIFE

HOW ARE YOU enjoying retirement?" I asked a couple who had recently settled in South Carolina. "Oh, I hardly ever see him," the wife quickly remarked. "He's up before breakfast poring over the pages of *The Wall Street Journal.* Then he's off to his stock broker's office all morning. We even had to buy another television set so he could watch the financial channel in the afternoon." She concluded, "He's obsessed with trying to make our money grow."

Finances are vital, but they must never become the tail that wags the dog. In the words of Norwegian playwright Henrik Ibsen, "Building one's life on a foundation of gold is just like building a house on a foundation of sand."

Building Fences

People everywhere treat the world as their personal possession. Henry David Thoreau wrote in his journal, "I am amused to see from my window how busily man has divided and staked off his domain. God must smile at these puny fences running hither and thither everywhere over the land."

The psalmist gives this warning:

*Do not trust in oppression, nor vainly
hope in robbery; if riches increase,
do not set your heart on them.*
— Psalm 62:10

We Are Caretakers

Every large philanthropic foundation has trustees who are selected to administer the funds. You and I are trustees, too. God's wealth has been presented to us "in trust." We are looking after it on His behalf. We are not owners, but stewards — caretakers of the Lord's riches.

Unfortunately, the leadership of the church often sends mixed messages. "I'm confused," one man told me. "On Sunday morning we are admonished to shun materialism, but on Monday morning the pastor is playing golf with the wealthiest member of the congregation."

There is something far more valuable than the original paintings on your wall or the exquisite jewels in your safe deposit box. Make the driving force of your ambition to bless the lives of others and you will be rich — regardless of your possessions.

*Riches are not forever, nor does
a crown endure to all generations.*
— Proverbs 27:24

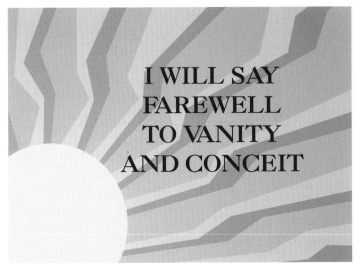

I WILL SAY FAREWELL TO VANITY AND CONCEIT

A YOUNG ATTORNEY who had just finished law school opened his practice just south of San Francisco. The day he opened his one-man office a gentleman walked through the door.

Wanting to make a good impression, the young lawyer picked up the phone and pretended to sound rather important. "Yes, we'll be taking those depositions in the morning. I received the forensic work today."

Then he placed his hand over the receiver and turned to the man he thought was a potential client and said, "Good morning. May help you?"

"No. I'm from the phone company. I came to connect your service."

A Pail of Water

There are moments when each of us could use a strong dose of humility. Best-selling inspirational writer, Og Mandino, says, "The next time you are tempted to boast, just place your fist in a full pail of water, and when you remove it, the hole remaining will give you a correct measure of your importance."

It's far better to let your accomplishments speak for themselves. As Will Rogers recommended, "Get someone else to blow your horn, and the sound will carry twice as far."

He was following the advice found in the Old Testament:

> *Let another praise you, and not*
> *your own mouth; someone else,*
> *and not your own lips.*
> *— Proverbs 27:2, NIV*

Enough About Me!

I'm certain you have been in the company of someone who found it impossible to stop talking about himself. I heard the story of a recording artist who was having dinner with a friend. For more than an hour he bragged about what people had been saying about his new release. At the end of the meal he said, "Enough about me. Now let's talk about you. What did you think of my last album?"

Everyone needs a certain amount of self-assurance to succeed, but to keep confidence from turning to conceit, make a commitment that you will elevate others, not yourself.

> *Pride goes before destruction, and*
> *a haughty spirit before a fall.*
> *— Proverbs 16:18*

I PROMISE
TO DEVELOP
A SYSTEMATIC
READING
PROGRAM

THE FAMOUS FRENCH writer, Balzac, after spending an evening with friends in shallow conversation, returned to his home and went straight to his study. He took off his coat, rubbed his hands and, looking at the books of the masters on the shelves, said, "Now for some real people!"

I remember having lunch with Charles "Tremendous" Jones, a dynamic motivational speaker from Pennsylvania. For years he has preached this message: "You will be the same in five years as you are today except for the people you meet and the books you read."

A Rich Reservoir

If you have children, do everything in your power to make reading central in their lives. One father, instead of giving his son an allowance, paid him one dollar for every self-help book he read. Later, the dad said, "If I had known ahead of time what those books would do for my son, I would have been glad to pay him much more."

The words you devour are more than mere ink on paper. They become a rich, permanent reservoir from which you will continually draw. It's sad that some people earn a college degree and feel their need for "book learning" is over. Without realizing it, their conversation soon becomes mundane and their mind settles into a predictable rut.

Schedule a specific time every day for reading. View it as being as vital as eating or sleeping — not as an optional or spare time activity. Personally, I concentrate on three areas:

1. God's Word

2. Self-help and inspiration

3. Skill building

The first builds character, the second motivates and the third develops talent.

It's Alive!

If you make a commitment to read the Bible for ten minutes every day, do it religiously. Some days it may be a struggle, but at other times you will become so stimulated and inspired that you will read for hours. You'll agree with Martin Luther, who wrote, "The Bible is alive, it speaks to me; it has feet, it runs after me; it has hands, it lays hold on me."

Whether you read for information, inspiration, enjoyment or personal growth, make reading a systematic, permanent part of your life.

Your word is a lamp to my feet
and a light to my path.
— Psalm 119:105

I COMMIT TO A LIFETIME OF PERSONAL GROWTH

THERE IS A great scene in *Alice in Wonderland* when Alice asks the Cheshire cat, "Will you tell me please, which way I ought to go from here?"

"That," the grinning cat replies, "depends a good deal on where you want to get to."

Define your mission clearly. It is the key to a lifetime of personal development.

Time for Action

What are the ingredients for growth? The apostle Peter says, "Add to your faith virtue, to virtue knowledge, to knowledge self-control, to self-control perseverance, to perseverance godliness, to godliness brotherly kindness, and to brotherly kindness love" (2 Peter 1:5-7).

Achievement requires more than positive thinking or good intentions. It requires action. In the words of a Chinese proverb, "I hear, and I forget; I see, and I remember; I do, and I understand."

Build on the talent you have, not what may interest you at a particular moment. As English writer Samuel Johnson said, "A man may be so much of everything that he is nothing of anything."

Be sure your vision is large enough to present a great challenge. In the office of a real estate developer I saw a plaque with these words:

> *"If you have accomplished all*
> *that you have planned for yourself*
> *— you have not planned enough."*

Beating the Odds

Continual progress is not as arduous as some people would have you believe. To be on the plus side of the ledger you only have to succeed 51 percent of the time. When you achieve more than that, consider it a bonus.

Resist the temptation to reach a plateau and level off. Someone wisely observed, "People don't grow old. They *become* old from not growing."

There are dozens of things you can do in one day for personal growth. For example, you can eat a healthy diet for a day. You can be an optimist for a day. You can encourage others for a day.

Why not do them for a week? Why not a month? Why not for a year? Yes, you can do them for a lifetime.

> *A wise man will hear and*
> *increase learning, and a man of*
> *understanding will attain wise counsel.*
> *— Proverbs 1:5*

Promise #74

I WILL RECOGNIZE AND REMOVE THE CAUSES OF STRESS

THE MANAGER OF a high-tech company told how his subordinates always came into his office upset about one thing or another. After listening to people he told them to leave a written report on his desk. Then, as they were about to walk out the door, he would say, "Don't forget rule six." He had said this many times, yet no one asked him to explain.

One day a young employee said, "Rule six. Yes, of course." He turned to leave the office, stopped and asked, "What is rule six?"

The manager explained, "Rule six is as follows: Don't take yourself too seriously."

The young man replied, "Thank you, sir. I'll remember that. But what are the other rules?"

"There are no other rules," exclaimed the manager.

A Matter of Balance

Millions of people face each day with clenched jaws,

wrinkled foreheads and knotted stomachs — totally stressed about things that are often beyond their control.

I like this observation that was printed in a medical journal:

> *"We come into this world head first*
> *and go out feet first; in between*
> *it's all a matter of balance."*

Coping With Pressure

Here are six principles to follow when you feel stressed:

1. Concentrate on doing one thing at a time.

2. Do your best without worrying about the outcome.

3. Don't fret about situations over which you have no control.

4. Treat the root cause of stress.

5. Face every crisis immediately.

6. Ask for the Lord's help. Jesus said, "Come to me, all you who are weary and burdened, and I will give you rest" (Matthew 11:28, NIV).

> *But He knows the way that*
> *I take; when He has tested me,*
> *I shall come forth as gold.*
> *— Job 23:10*

I WILL PRACTICE THE RULES OF GOOD NUTRITION

A NUTRITIONIST IN San Diego has found a way to get a head start on improving the diets of her patients. On the first visit she weighs a patient and presents a two week diary. "I want you to write down every bite of food you eat — including the amount."

Two weeks later, on the second appointment, she reports the average patient has already lost between eight and ten pounds and is practicing better rules of nutrition. "The quickest way to solve a problem is to *recognize* it," she says.

Food Tampering

Charles Kuntzleman, noted health consultant and author of *The Well Family Book,* says, "Many Christians believe that we are permitted to eat whatever we want. But it does not give us license to consume an excess of real or imitation foods." He states, "Yes, if God made it, it is good. But if man has tampered with it, beware."

My wife and I recently had dinner with Cheryl Townsley, author of *Food Smart*. In her book she writes that over two million people die annually from all causes and diet plays a role in 68 percent of the cases. She adds, "If you remove suicide and unintentional injuries such as auto accidents from the list of causes, the number of deaths to which diet is a factor is a whopping 80 percent."

Paul declared that our bodies are God's, not ours.

> *Do you not know that your body*
> *is a temple of the Holy Spirit, who*
> *is in you, whom you have received*
> *from God? You are not your own;*
> *you were bought at a price. Therefore*
> *honor God with your body.*
> — *1 Corinthians 6:19-20, NIV*

The Answer

If I were to ask you to recommend a healthier, more nutritious diet, you would probably tell me what health professionals have been telling you for years: "Eat more fruits, vegetables and grains, and consume less fat and sugar."

Since you already know the answers, what are you waiting for?

> *"Nevertheless He did not leave*
> *Himself without witness, in that*
> *He did good, gave us rain from*
> *heaven and fruitful seasons, filling*
> *our hearts with food and gladness."*
> — *Acts 14:17*

I PROMISE TO KEEP MYSELF PHYSICALLY FIT

YOU CAN HAVE the greatest objectives in the world, but what good are visions if you lack the strength to accomplish them?

Bill Hybels, pastor of Willow Creek Community Church near Chicago, observes, "A lot of people these days are run down physically. Most have no idea how much their physical condition undermines their attempts to love others. They fail to realize that it takes physical energy to listen, to serve, to confront, to rebuke."

According to Hybels, "People who are out to shape tend to be easily irritated, critical, defensive and negative. It's hard for them to love others, and it's equally hard for others to love them."

A Long Walk

Jesus knew the importance of bodily strength. He was a carpenter before power tools were invented and was strong enough to walk fifty miles over rugged terrain to Tyre and

Sidon. His work on earth was highly focused on the physical condition of man. Almost 20 percent of the four Gospels deal with His healing ministry.

Everyone knows the benefits of exercise, but many seek it in the wrong places. On the bulletin board of a YMCA, someone posted this message:

> *"The only exercise some people get*
> *is jumping to conclusions, running*
> *down their friends, sidestepping*
> *responsibility, dodging issues, passing*
> *the buck and pushing their luck."*

The Fifteen-Minute Commitment

One simple decision, if kept, can have a dramatic effect on your longevity. Make a commitment to spend fifteen minutes a day in physical exercise. Your routine may be walking, jogging or using that special piece of equipment you bought on an impulse from a television commercial.

If possible, ask an expert for guidance. It's been said that "practice makes perfect," but a tennis player who practices an incorrect stroke may lose in more ways than one. Even a basic exercise such as doing sit-ups can produce more harm than help if not performed properly.

A corporate health trainer suggests, "Aim for a well-balanced program that will strengthen your heart and lungs, build your muscles, increase your flexibility and produce the correct weight/height ratio." What's the best advice? Get started!

> *I praise you because I am*
> *fearfully and wonderfully made;*
> *your works are wonderful.*
> *— Psalm 139:14, NIV*

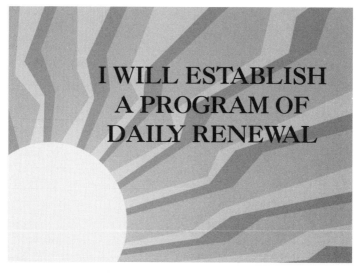

I WILL ESTABLISH
A PROGRAM OF
DAILY RENEWAL

FOLLOWING THEIR RELEASE, prisoners of war have shared inspiring stories of how they renewed their spirit and hope. Author Denis Waitley tells about Air Force Colonel George Hall who played an imaginary round of golf each day during his seven years as a POW in North Vietnam. Says Waitley, "Those mental exercises paid off when he got back to the real thing. After seven golf-less years, he was back in form in less than one month after his release. He played to his four-stroke handicap in the Pro-Am preliminary to the $125,000 Greater New Orleans Open."

What's Your Secret?

How do you prepare to face a new day?

At a seminar I conducted on self-motivation, I asked those in the audience to tell me their secrets of daily renewal. The comments included: "I avoid reading the paper until later in the day. There are too many negative headlines." "I read promises from Psalms and Proverbs." "When I need a lift, I mentally recount the best moments of my life." "When I go to bed, I also put my troubles to sleep."

The word *motive,* from which we get *motivation,* is defined as that which comes from within — not from without. Scripture affirms:

> *Even though our outward man*
> *is perishing, yet the inward man*
> *is being renewed day by day.*
> *— 2 Corinthians 4:16*

No More Coasting

Without a plan to rejuvenate your spirits, you lose your thrust and drive. As a friend once told me, "If you are coasting, you're either losing momentum or else you are headed downhill."

Anytime is a good time to refresh and quicken your mind — before you get up, while you take a shower, when you are driving to work, during a lunch break, taking a walk after dinner or in your easy chair before retiring for the evening.

Forget the troubles of yesterday. Say, "It happened, and I am better and wiser because of it."

The Lord gives you a new day so you can become a new person. He has done His part, now you can do yours.

> *And do not be conformed to this world,*
> *but be transformed by the renewing of your*
> *mind, that you may prove what is that good*
> *and acceptable and perfect will of God.*
> *— Romans 12:2*

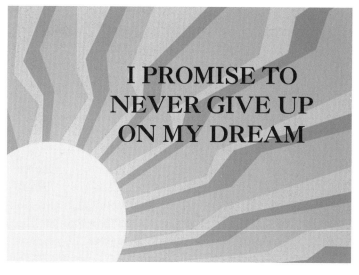

I PROMISE TO
NEVER GIVE UP
ON MY DREAM

IN ATLANTA, WHILE I was autographing books at a convention, a young man received his signed copy and said, "Thanks! I hope you live to see all your dreams come true."

I smiled and answered, "I appreciate that, but if they all came true I'd probably be dead. As long as I have a dream, I'm alive!"

He Wouldn't Quit

Achievement requires more than a vision — it takes tenacity.

The manager of a restaurant was surprised to see a young waiter he had fired return to his job. "Didn't you get my letter?" the boss inquired. "Yes sir," he answered. "On the inside it said, 'You're fired!' On the outside it read, 'Return in five days,' so here I am." That's perseverance.

Captain James Cook, the English explorer, faced monumental obstacles, but he kept sailing on. Said the captain,

"I had ambition not only to go farther than any man had ever been before, but as far as it was possible for a man to go."

You don't have to travel alone. Allow the Lord to be your navigator. The apostle Paul wrote to Timothy:

> *I know whom I have believed and am*
> *persuaded that He is able to keep what I*
> *have committed to Him until that Day.*
> *— 2 Timothy 1:12*

Wake Up!

"What's the first thing you should do to make your dreams come true?" a kindergarten teacher asked her class.

A little boy raised his hand and answered, "Wake yourself up!" He was right.

We need the belief and optimism of Annie, the little girl with red hair who sings, "Oh, the sun will come out, tomorrow!" It's only a day away!

Remember, people will never see the target at which you are aiming — only the target you hit.

> *And let us not grow weary while doing*
> *good, for in due season we shall*
> *reap if we do not lose heart.*
> *— Galatians 6:9*

IV.

PROMISES TO MY WORLD

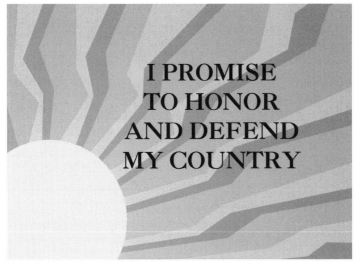

I PROMISE TO HONOR AND DEFEND MY COUNTRY

W HEN GOD CREATED all things He brought into being an orderly universe and later ordained government for all people.

At Mount Sinai, after God rescued His children out of slavery in Egypt, He organized them into a nation. He constituted them "a kingdom of priests" (Exodus 19:6) with Himself as their ruler. There were administrative, judicial and military responsibilities.

Pledging Allegiance

Today, while we have earthly rulers, we continue to recognize that we are "under God." Our founding president, George Washington, stated, "It is impossible to rightly govern the world without God and the Bible."

When the president and other federal employees take their oath of office, they do so by placing their hand on the Holy Bible and pledging their loyalty to both God and country.

I still remember starting every school day with my hand over my heart reciting, "I pledge allegiance to the flag of the United States of America and to the republic for which it stands, one nation under God, indivisible, with liberty and justice for all."

When Jesus was asked whether we are to serve God or man, He declared, "Render therefore to Caesar the things that are Caesar's, and to God the things that are God's" (Matthew 22:21).

Peter gave this directive to all believers:

> *Submit yourselves to every ordinance*
> *of man for the Lord's sake, whether to*
> *the king as supreme, or to governors,*
> *as to those who are sent by him for*
> *the punishment of evildoers and for*
> *the praise of those who do good.*
> *—1 Peter 2:13-14*

Under Appointment

Charles Colson, author and a former government official, recognizes the vital role of law in our lives. He observes, "The state is not a remedy for sin, but a means to restrain it."

When you promise to honor and defend your country you are fulfilling the will of God.

> *Let every soul be subject to the governing*
> *authorities. For there is no authority*
> *except from God, and the authorities*
> *that exist are appointed by God.*
> *—Romans 13:1*

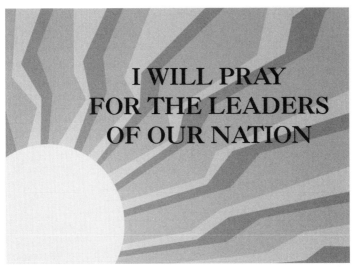

I WILL PRAY FOR THE LEADERS OF OUR NATION

AT HIS INAUGURATION as president in January 1961, John F. Kennedy challenged the nation with these words: "Ask not what your country can do for you — ask what you can do for your country."

Regardless of our occupation or status in life, there is one thing each of us can do. We can pray. As individuals, or in larger groups we can flood the president, congress, the supreme court justices and our local government leaders with fervent prayer. In the words of author E. M. Bounds, "Talking to men for God is a great thing but talking to God for men is greater still."

The Road of Intercession

Prayer takes many forms. We can have *communion* with the Lord; we can *petition* Him with our specific personal requests, or we can practice *intercession,* praying that God will give wisdom and guidance to others.

Dick Eastman, in his book *No Easy Road,* says,

"Intercession engages in conflict with a million evils facing our fellowmen. An intercession must bid farewell to self and welcome the burdens of humanity. In truth, the climax of prayer is intercession."

God would not have anointed kings if He did not mean for them to rule according to His principles. The Word declares:

> *He changes the times and the seasons;*
> *He removes kings and raises up kings; He*
> *gives wisdom to the wise and knowledge*
> *to those who have understanding.*
> *— Daniel 2:21*

Touching God

What should be our prayer for those who lead our land?

- Pray for wisdom — that they may perceive and know what is best.

- Pray for guidance — that they would fulfill God's will.

- Pray for security — that the Lord would provide for their safety.

- Pray for peace — that they may foster reconciliation and accord.

> *I exhort first of all that supplications,*
> *prayers, intercessions, and giving of*
> *thanks be made for all men, for kings*
> *and all who are in authority, that we*
> *may lead a quiet and peaceable life*
> *in all godliness and reverence.*
> *— 1 Timothy 2:1-2*

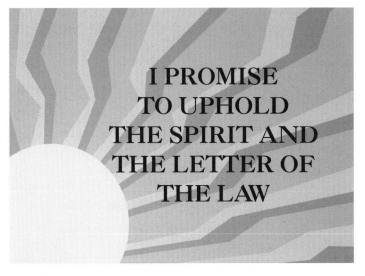

I PROMISE TO UPHOLD THE SPIRIT AND THE LETTER OF THE LAW

MANY PEOPLE BELIEVE that law is subject to their own interpretation. An employee at a lumber company was arrested for building his entire home with materials he had stolen piece by piece from his workplace over a two-year period. At his trial, he explained, "I asked for a raise and didn't get it. I only took what I felt was owed to me!"

In Texas, a highway patrolman said he's heard dozens of excuses from people he has stopped for speeding. He even had a man who led him on a high speed chase to a gas station. The speeder jumped out and ran to the restroom shouting, "I didn't think I was going to make it!"

Instant Judgment

When it comes to right and wrong, situation ethics won't do. Deep inside we know whether our actions are honest or evil, just or unjust, and the price of deceit comes sooner than we think.

For too long people have attempted to divert the blame and shirk their responsibility. Ronald Reagan stated, "We must reject the idea that every time a law is broken, society is guilty rather than the lawbreaker. It is time to restore the American precept that each individual is accountable for his actions."

Back to Basics

Man has produced over forty million laws but has yet to improve on the Ten Commandments. In fact, the Bible contains the basic principles of law. They include:

- All crimes are ultimately crimes against God.

- We are personally responsible for our behavior.

- We are to respect human life.

- The punishment must be equal to the offense.

- There is universal justice.

Theodore Roosevelt once wrote, "No man is above the law and no man is below it; nor do we ask any man's permission when we ask him to obey it." Commit yourself to live both by the letter and the spirit of the law.

*"But this is the covenant that I
will make with the house of Israel
after those days, says the Lord: I
will put My law in their minds, and
write it on their hearts; and I will be
their God, and they shall be My people."
— Jeremiah 31:33*

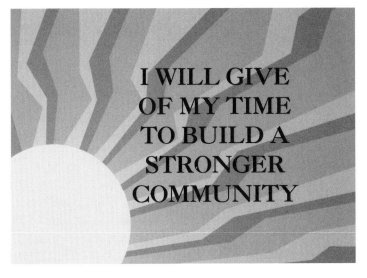

I WILL GIVE
OF MY TIME
TO BUILD A
STRONGER
COMMUNITY

T HE QUALITY OF life you expect from your city or neighborhood is not a matter of happenstance. It is a result of thousands of man-hours by volunteers who tackle everything from picking up litter along roadways to being members of the school board.

This, however, only scratches the surface of the real need.

Time for a Change

"The massive buildup of the welfare system in America has been a tragedy," a social worker once told me. "The recipient is trapped by dependency, and millions have been denied the privilege of personally reaching out to those in need."

There is a growing chorus of voices who believe it is time for churches, local agencies and individuals to once again assume their role to rescue the perishing and care for the dying.

Saint Augustine asked, "What does love look like? It has the hands to help others. It has the feet to hasten to the poor and needy. It has the eyes to see misery and want. It has the ears to hear the sighs and sorrows of men. That is what love looks like."

Every community needs continual renewal. In the voice of Mother Teresa:

"To keep a lamp burning we
have to keep putting oil in it."

The Measuring Stick

I once heard a city councilman ask, "How many hours did you give to your community last year? One? Ten? One hundred?" Then he added, "We need more than your taxes, we desperately need your talent."

Some of the most rewarding moments of my life have been my involvement with the Voluntary Action Center, Rotary International, Junior Achievement and the United Way.

The true measure of a community is not the number of office buildings, the miles of paved roads or the size of its utility company. It is best measured by the time and assistance we give to those we call our neighbors.

"'You shall love the Lord your God with
all your heart, with all your soul, with all
your strength, and with all your mind,'
and 'your neighbor as yourself.'"
— Luke 10:27

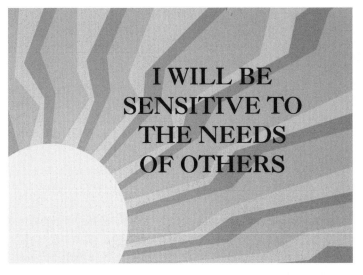

I WILL BE SENSITIVE TO THE NEEDS OF OTHERS

LONG AGO, A man wandering through a barren desert suddenly came upon a spring of cool, crystal-clear water. It was so refreshing that he decided to take the king a sample of it. He filled his canteen and began his long trek through the hot sands until he reached the palace. On the journey, however, the water became stale because of the old leather canteen in which it was stored.

The king cordially accepted the gift of this faithful citizen. He tasted it with an expression of deep appreciation and pleasure. The wanderer left, his heart filled with delight.

When the man departed, several men in the king's court tasted the putrid water and asked the king, "Why did you pretend to enjoy it?"

"Ah," responded the king, "it was not the water I tasted but the spirit in which it was given."

Are you sensitive to the needs of others — emotionally, spiritually and physically? Do you recognize when others are hurting, or are you too self-absorbed to care? Nick

Coleman, a newspaper columnist from Minnesota, observes, "Somewhere at our core, men need to believe in something greater than Monday night football, stock car racing and whiskey."

There *is* something greater. You can open your heart to those in distress.

> *Do not forget to entertain*
> *strangers, for by so doing some*
> *have unwittingly entertained angels.*
> *— Hebrews 13:2*

The Best Bet

In Arkansas, an usher at a racetrack took his life savings of seven thousand dollars out of the bank, and he gave it to his nephew to help the young man pay his way through college. The man was asked, "How can you afford to do something like that?"

He smiled and responded, "Every day I watch thousands of men bet on horses and lose their shirts. The way I figure it, a man might stand a chance to make a killing if he bets on a human being."

What investment are you ready to make?

> *But whoever has this world's goods,*
> *and sees his brother in need, and*
> *shuts up his heart from him, how*
> *does the love of God abide in him?*
> *— 1 John 3:17*

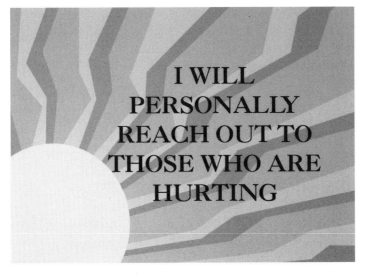

I WILL PERSONALLY REACH OUT TO THOSE WHO ARE HURTING

WHEN BILL WILSON was fourteen, he and his distraught mother sat down on a curb over a drainage ditch in St. Petersburg, Florida. "You wait here," she told him as she left — never to return.

Three days later, Bill was still sitting on that curb when Dave Rudenis, a man who lived down the street, saw his plight and walked over to him. He brought Bill something to eat and offered to pay his registration fee for a youth camp that week. It was the beginning of a dramatic turn-around in the young man's life.

Today, Bill Wilson is in Bushwick, a drug infested "war zone" in Brooklyn where over eleven thousand children are reached each week in the Metro Church he established to help kids just like himself. You can read his dramatic story in his book, *Whose Child Is This?*

Says Bill, "I don't even want to think about what my life would have become if Dave had not seen the need."

In the words of Jesus, "Assuredly, I say to you, inasmuch as you did it to one of the least of these My brethren, you did it to Me" (Matthew 25:40).

International evangelist Luis Palau recalls meeting a Methodist minister who worked in the inner-city of Bristol, England. When asked what he did there, he replied, "I minister to the last, the least, the lonely and the lost." It needs to be our mission, too. As John Bunyan wrote in *Pilgrim's Progress:*

> *"He who bestows his goods*
> *upon the poor, shall have as*
> *much again, and ten times more."*

Cross the Tracks

A reporter asked noted mental health specialist, Karl Menninger, "What advice would you give to a person who feels a nervous breakdown coming on?"

The answer the journalist expected was, "Consult a psychiatrist." However, that's not how Menninger replied. Instead he said, "Lock up your house, go across the railway tracks, find someone in need and do something to help that person."

We need to reach the conclusion of a bank executive who drove through an impoverished area: "I wondered why somebody didn't do something," he said. "Then I realized that I was that somebody."

> *"And whoever gives one of these little ones*
> *only a cup of cold water in the name of a*
> *disciple, assuredly, I say to you, he shall*
> *by no means lose his reward."*
> *— Matthew 10:42*

I PROMISE
TO SUPPORT
THOSE WHO
MINISTER
TO PEOPLE
IN NEED

MEETING A GREAT need is comparable to fighting a major battle. For every soldier with a rifle on the front lines, there are countless more at home who play a vital supporting role.

Your calling in life may be to become the best engineer, school teacher or graphic artist possible. What you do behind the scenes, however, may allow a cause to be championed or a crusade to go forward.

Flour and Oil

When the head of a high-profile outreach was criticized in the press, a major donor was asked, "Do you plan to continue your support?"

"I've never even thought of withdrawing my finances," he answered, "I don't give *to* a ministry, I give *through* a ministry."

People may come and go, but we have an obligation to sustain the work God has established.

Providing for the well-being of God's servants is part of His plan to meet human need. The prophet Elijah was not only fed by the ravens, he was told, "Arise, go to Zarephath, which belongs to Sidon, and dwell there. See, I have commanded a widow there to provide for you" (1 Kings 17:9).

All the woman had was a little flour and some oil, but that was enough. God told him to announce:

> *The jar of flour will not be used up*
> *and the jug of oil will not run dry until*
> *the day the Lord gives rain on the land.*
> *— 1 Kings 17:14, NIV*

Worthy Workers

The pattern for the support of those in ministry was established by Christ. When He sent out the twelve disciples, He told them, "Provide neither gold nor silver nor copper in your moneybelts, nor bag for your journey, nor two tunics, nor sandals, nor staffs; for a worker is worthy of his food" (Matthew 10:9-10).

As the disciples traveled from village to village, their financial needs were met. In one instance, "Joanna the wife of Cuza, the manager of Herod's household; Susanna; and many others. These women were helping to support them out of their own means" (Luke 8:3, NIV).

Make a heavy burden light. Give strength to those who provide strength.

> *Let him who is taught the word share in all*
> *good things with him who teaches.*
> *— Galatians 6:6*

V.

PROMISES TO GOD

I PROMISE TO PLACE THE LORD FIRST IN EVERY ASPECT OF MY LIFE

FORMER PASTOR, H. A. Ironside, of the Moody Church in Chicago, told the story of an American Indian who was giving the testimony of his conversion to a gathering of members of his tribe.

The new believer explained that in the beginning he was so happy in knowing his Savior, he felt as though he would never sin again. As time went on, however, he became conscious of an inner conflict, which he described as follows:

> *"It seems, my brothers, that I have two dogs fighting in my heart. One is a very kind dog that is always watching out for my best interest. The other is a very bad, ugly dog who is always trying to destroy everything that is good. These dogs give me much trouble because they are always quarreling and fighting with each other."*

One of his fellow tribesmen looked up and asked, "Which one wins?"

The new convert instantly replied, "Whichever one I say 'Sic em' to!"

Who holds first place in our lives? It is the one we choose.

The apostle Paul described the battle, "For the sinful nature desires what is contrary to the Spirit, and the Spirit what is contrary to the sinful nature. They are in conflict with each other, so that you do not do what you want" Galatians 5:17, NIV).

What's the answer? The Word declares:

> *Live by the Spirit, and you will not*
> *gratify the desire of the sinful nature.*
> *— Galatians 5:16, NIV*

Competing Forces

At any given moment there are dozens of forces vying for our attention — from our friends to the constant bombardment of the media.

The only way to create order out of chaos is to make a decision regarding our priorities. Without question, that order must be God first, family second and everything else after that. Oswald Chambers says, "If we build to please ourselves, we are building on the sand; if we build for the love of God, we are building on the rock."

Of the commandments the Almighty gave to Moses, which was delivered first? "You shall have no other gods before me" (Exodus 20:3, NIV).

Make God's priority yours.

> *For it is God who works in you both*
> *to will and to do for His good pleasure.*
> *— Philippians 2:13*

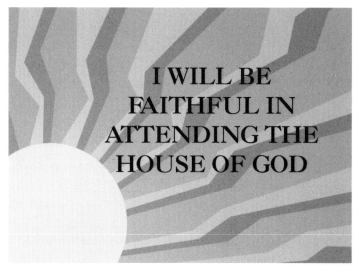

I WILL BE FAITHFUL IN ATTENDING THE HOUSE OF GOD

ONE MORNING THE telephone rang in the pastor's office of the Washington church where the U.S. president attended. An eager voice inquired, "Tell me, do you expect the president to be in church this Sunday?"

"That I can't promise," replied the minister, "but we expect God to be here, and we believe that should be incentive enough for a good attendance."

Dozens of Excuses

In most places of worship the membership roll far exceeds the number who are present each Sunday. Why? The pastor of a small church in San Diego shared a few of the excuses he has heard.

"They keep the temperature too cold, and it hurts my arthritis." "As long as Mr. Smith is a deacon, I'm not sure I can sit in the same building with him. He's a scoundrel." "We are working so many hours that Sunday morning is the only time I can spend with my family." The minister concluded, "People can find plenty of excuses but no reasons."

Scripture tells us that we are to encourage fellowship — "not forsaking the assembling of ourselves together, as is the manner of some, but exhorting one another, and so much the more as you see the Day approaching" (Hebrews 10:25).

What Will I Give?

The church is only a building unless it comes to life by both God's presence and yours. As A. W. Tozer stated, "One hundred religious persons knit together into a unity by careful organization does not constitute a church any more than eleven dead men make a football team. The first requisite is life, always."

Don't ask, "What will I receive from the service?" Ask, "What will I give?"

Why is our attendance so important? When we are not physically present in God's house, it disheartens the minister, discourages fellow members and weakens the body of Christ and the church's impact in the community.

When the doors of the sanctuary are open, be there — for all the right reasons.

And they continued steadfastly in the
apostles' doctrine and fellowship, in the
breaking of bread, and in prayers.
— Acts 2:42

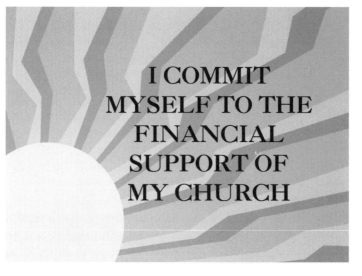

I COMMIT
MYSELF TO THE
FINANCIAL
SUPPORT OF
MY CHURCH

O N A JOURNEY to Israel I visited the Sea of Galilee — a fresh lake that is brimming with life. It is alive because it gives out a portion of all it receives, flowing into the river Jordan.

At the south end of the Jordan is the Dead Sea; the saltiest body of water in the world. It bears that name because there is no outlet; it keeps all it receives and can sustain no animal life.

Giving keeps us dynamic and alive. In the analogy of Billy Graham, "God has given us two hands — one to receive with and other to give with. We are not cisterns made for hoarding; we are channels made for sharing."

Hand Me a Shovel

We do not give to receive, yet that's the way it always seems to turn out.

A generous supporter of God's work was once asked, "How do you manage to give so much?"

He responded, "The Lord never stops shoveling good things on me. If I didn't shovel it back, I'd be buried in an avalanche."

He was obeying God's directive: "On the first day of the week let each one of you lay something aside, storing up as he may prosper" (1 Corinthians 16:2).

In 1419 an epitaph was written for Edward Earl of Devonshire that still rings true:

> *"What we gave, we have; what we spent,*
> *we had; what we kept, we lost."*

Good Night's Sleep

The founder of Methodism, John Wesley, taught that a faithful servant should have three objectives regarding finances: "Make all you can. Save all you can. Give all you can."

It has been said that the world is full of two kinds of people, the givers and the takers. The takers eat well, but the givers sleep well.

Keep your river of life flowing. Give.

> *"Bring all the tithes into the storehouse,*
> *that there may be food in My house,*
> *and try Me now in this," says the Lord*
> *of hosts, "If I will not open for you the*
> *windows of heaven and pour out for*
> *you such blessing, that there will not*
> *be room enough to receive it."*
> *— Malachi 3:10*

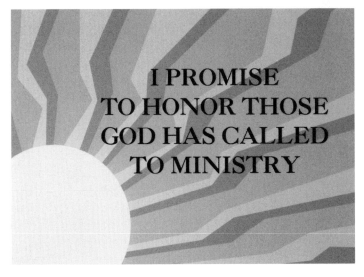

**I PROMISE
TO HONOR THOSE
GOD HAS CALLED
TO MINISTRY**

I T MUST BE nice to work only one day a week," a parishioner half-jokingly said to his pastor. Tired of hearing that sentiment, the minister quickly replied, "Actually, I work for the church all week and donate my time on Sunday."

The truth is that most ministers live under severe stress. They are not only carrying their own burdens but assume those of many in their congregation.

Unfinished Business

"When I was asked to be the pastor," said one exhausted clergyman, "the board told me, 'We believe you should have all the time you need each week for personal prayer and preparation for your pulpit ministry.'"

Later, when he was under doctor's orders to take a two month leave of absence, the minister said, "They forgot to tell me I was expected to be a full-time administrator, keep a busy counseling schedule, make regular hospital and home visits, be involved in the community, serve the denomination and make time for dozens more activities from marrying and burying to personal evangelism."

David Sawyer, a Presbyterian minister says, "Whenever I find myself feeling guilty over unfinished business, I tell myself that only Jesus was able to say, 'It is finished!'"

We Salute You!

We should do everything within our power to lift the heavy load of those in ministry. The Word declares:

> *And we urge you, brethren, to*
> *recognize those who labor among*
> *you, and are over you in the Lord and*
> *admonish you, and to esteem them very*
> *highly in love for their work's sake.*
> *— 1 Thessalonians 5:12-13*

A graduate of the U.S. Naval Academy told me, "The greatest lesson I learned while in training was that you don't salute the man, you salute his uniform. The greater the number of stripes he wears, the greater honor he deserves."

Those who stand behind the sacred desk deserve our high esteem and admiration. They are God's representatives, and how we treat them is a mirror of our honor for the Lord.

> *Let the elders who rule well be counted*
> *worthy of double honor, especially those*
> *who labor in the word and doctrine.*
> *— 1 Timothy 5:17*

Promise #90

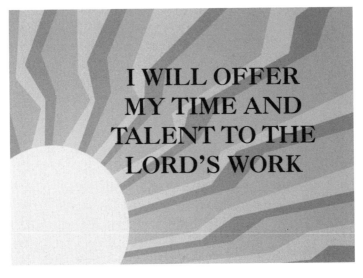

I WILL OFFER MY TIME AND TALENT TO THE LORD'S WORK

MAMMOTH CAVE, KENTUCKY, is one of the world's largest known cave systems. Running through the cavern is the Echo River which is filled with strange creatures — blind beetles, crayfish and even an eyeless fish that's about three inches long.

Why are these creatures sightless? Because in the darkness of the cave they didn't use what God originally gave to them.

Just as an unused automobile becomes rusty and an untended garden is soon choked with weeds, talents that are latent and not exercised will one day fade away.

Capture the Power

God created plants and trees with limited characteristics and possibilities, but that's not how he made you and me. We have unlimited potential. If we can imagine it, chances are we will achieve it.

The first time I saw Niagara Falls I was overwhelmed at

the might and force being unleashed. For centuries, huge amounts of water flowed over the falls, but today that power has been harnessed. The falls now drive one of the world's largest hydroelectric facilities, producing over twenty-two million kilowatts of power. It supplies light and energy to the entire region.

The Lord also sees the hidden strength and talent that you possess to be used for His kingdom.

Do not present your members
as instruments of unrighteousness to sin,
but present yourselves to God as being
alive from the dead, and your members
as instruments of righteousness to God.
— Romans 6:13

The Masterpiece

When you hire a carpenter you don't ask, "How many tools do your have in your box?" You are only interested in one thing: Is he proficient with the tools he owns and does he care about his work? As John Ruskin wrote, "When love and skill work together, expect a masterpiece." Remember, the Lord is looking for two things: ability and availability. He is depending on your time and talent to accomplish His work.

For you were bought at a price;
therefore glorify God in your body
and in your spirit, which are God's.
— 1 Corinthians 6:20

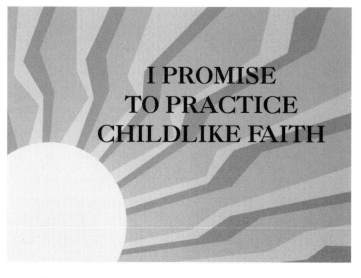

I PROMISE TO PRACTICE CHILDLIKE FAITH

J C. PENNEY told how he overheard a conversation between his parents when his father was dying. His dad remarked, "I just know J. C. will make it."

From that day forward, Penney said he *felt* he would succeed in life. His father's trust and confidence in him never left his mind.

We have been taught all our lives that faith in God can move mighty mountains. You also need to know that God has faith in *you*. He believes in your potential and your promise.

Your Great Discovery

Faith is the key that unlocks the door to an unexpected dimension of living.

Richard Foster, author of *Celebration of Discipline,* believes, "The inner reality of the spiritual world is available to all who are willing to search for it. Often I have discovered that those who so freely debunk the spiritual world have never taken ten minutes to investigate whether or not such a world really exists."

Scripture teaches, "We do not look at the things which are seen, but at the things which are not seen. For the things which are seen are temporary, but the things which are not seen are eternal" (2 Corinthians 4:18).

Jesus gave His followers this powerful declaration:

> *"Therefore I say to you, whatever things*
> *you ask when you pray, believe that you*
> *receive them, and you will have them."*
> *— Mark 11:24*

Overcoming Obstacles

Logic, reasoning and scientific inquiry have their place, yet we are incomplete without a simple childlike faith and belief.

Author Frank K. Ellis states, "Every single one of us is handicapped — physically, mentally, socially and spiritually — to some degree, and although we seldom think about it, the person without *faith* has a far greater handicap than the person without *feet*."

You can rest assured that the same God who made you will sustain you. Every rung on His ladder to heaven will securely hold you until you are safe in His arms.

> *"Assuredly, I say to you, whoever*
> *does not receive the kingdom of God as*
> *a little child will by no means enter it."*
> *— Mark 10:15*

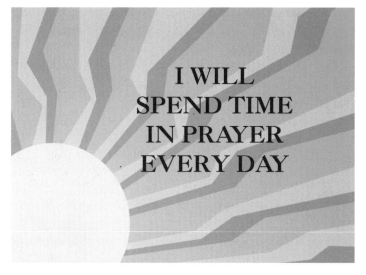

I WILL SPEND TIME IN PRAYER EVERY DAY

I RECALL HEARING the story of a little girl in Cincinnati who told her father at bedtime, "Daddy, I want you to say something to God — something I want to tell Him very much. I have such a tiny voice that I don't think He would hear me. But you have such a strong, loud voice, and He will surely hear you."

The father told his daughter that if need be, God would stop the sweetest music of the angels and say, "Hush! Stop singing for a while. There's a little girl in Cincinnati who wants to whisper something in My ear."

No matter what we say or how we say it — even if the thought is unspoken — we have a God who hears and answers prayer.

Out of the Shadows

In London, I saw the stage production of *Shadowlands,* the dramatic life story of C. S. Lewis. Concerning prayer, the great Christian academic said, "The moment you wake up each morning, all your wishes and hopes for the day rush at you like wild animals. And the first job each morning consists of shoving it all back; in listening to that other voice, taking that other point of view, letting that other, larger, stronger, quieter life come flowing in."

God not only hears your words, He knows your thoughts and is patiently waiting to respond. Through the prophet Isaiah, He declared:

> *Before they call I will answer; and while*
> *they are still speaking, I will hear.*
> *— Isaiah 65:24*

Keep the Lines Open

Make a vow to yourself and the Lord that you will spend time every day in prayer. Like God's servant, Daniel, determine that you will lift your voice to heaven morning, noon and night.

Don't wait for an emergency to call on the Lord. His number is not 911. Instead learn to pray without ceasing and stay plugged into God's information highway.

In the words of R. A. Torrey, "Pray for great things, expect great things, work for great things, but above all, pray."

> *"But you, when you pray, go into*
> *your room, and when you have shut*
> *your door, pray to your Father who*
> *is in the secret place; and your Father*
> *who sees in secret will reward you openly."*
> *— Matthew 6:6*

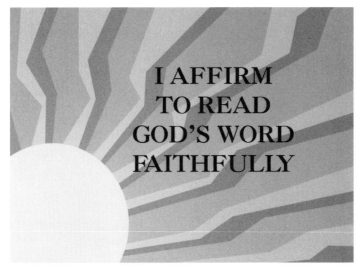

**I AFFIRM
TO READ
GOD'S WORD
FAITHFULLY**

OVER TWO HUNDRED Thousand Titles in Stock" boasted a sign at the entry of a New York City bookstore I visited recently. All the wisdom in those volumes combined is still no match for what is contained in the pages of the world's all-time best-selling book — the holy Bible. God's Word can be found in virtually every home in the nation. Unfortunately, just because it's present does not mean it is being read.

Day and Night

There are dozens of reasons for establishing a personal program of regular, consistent Bible reading. It isn't the suggestion of man but a directive of the Lord. He declared: "This Book of the Law shall not depart from your mouth, but you shall meditate in it day and night, that you may observe to do according to all that is written in it. For then you will make your way prosperous, and then you will have good success" (Joshua 1:8).

The same spirit that descended on those who wrote the Word will rest on you as you read it. As Dwight L. Moody exclaimed, "I know the Bible is inspired because it inspires me."

For decades there have been animated discussions of which version of God's Word should be read. I heard one man comment, "I refuse to read any translation of the Bible. I'm sticking with the King James Version." He didn't realize the KJV is also a translation of Scripture since the sixty-six books of the Bible were originally written in three separate languages: Hebrew, Aramaic and Greek.

Translations such as the New International Version and the New King James Version are widely acclaimed for both their faithfulness to the original language and ease of reading.

Be Specific

Here are four recommendations for making your Bible reading come alive:

1. *Read at a specific time.* Build time for the Word into your daily schedule.

2. *Read in a specific place.* Find a special location to get alone with your thoughts.

3. *Read with a specific plan.* Set your objectives and stick to your schedule.

4. *Read for understanding rather than speed.* Remember: It's important to get into the Word, but it's even more important to allow the Word to get into you.

> *Search the Scriptures, for in them*
> *you think you have eternal life; and*
> *these are they which testify of Me.*
> *— John 5:39*

MY LIFE WILL REFLECT MY BELIEF

W HEN JOHN ASHCROFT, now a United States senator, began his race for governor of the state of Missouri, he strongly opposed a proposed state lottery, yet the polls showed that 83 percent of Missourians were in favor of that form of gambling. His opponent, Gene McNary, supported the lottery, but Ashcroft still defeated McNary two to one in the primary.

During the November election the lottery won — and so did Ashcroft. I've known John since he was a young man, and he has always been a straight arrow — you always knew where he stood.

As one voter said, "I know that gambling has a great potential for abuse. I wanted someone to administer it that I could trust."

A Call to Action

Character counts. It has been said that one person with a belief is equal to a force of ninety-nine who only have interests. Belief is even more powerful when our convictions are transformed into action. We don't read about the *plans* or *intentions* of the apostles. Instead, the fifth book of the New Testament is named the *Acts of the Apostles*.

To emphasize the necessity of living what we believe, Jesus told the story of a man who was walking from Jerusalem to Jericho and fell among thieves who robbed him, stripped him of his clothing and left him half dead. People ignored the man's plight until the good Samaritan came by.

> *"And when he saw him, he took pity*
> *on him...and bandaged his wounds,*
> *pouring on oil and wine. Then he put*
> *the man on his own donkey, took him*
> *to an inn and took care of him."*
> *— Luke 10:33-34, NIV*

The Great Reflection

Our view of the world is often a mirror of ourselves. If we are generous, we expect our friends to be charitable. If we are greedy, we will be skeptical of others. If we are honest, we won't be looking for deceit.

The world will be a better place when our behavior reflects God's best.

> *For if you live according to the flesh you*
> *will die; but if by the Spirit you put to*
> *death the deeds of the body, you will live.*
> *— Romans 8:13*

I PROMISE TO SHARE THE GOOD NEWS

L AST YEAR, PRIOR to a high school graduation in California, the school board ruled that the name of God could not be mentioned during the ceremony.

At the graduation, in the middle of her speech, the valedictorian hesitated for a moment. Then she covered her mouth with her hand and sneezed. Immediately, in what proved to be a prearranged response, the entire senior class yelled, "God bless you!"

The audience broke into applause — everyone except the board members.

About two minutes later, the valedictorian sneezed again, and the response was repeated. The students were determined that the Lord would not be banned from their special day.

Under Appointment

When Lloyd Ogilvie was pastor of Hollywood Presbyterian Church, he didn't allow the congregation to call those on the staff "ministers." Said Ogilvie, "We want every member of the church to consider himself or herself a minister of God."

Each believer needs to echo the words of the apostle Paul, who wrote:

> *For if I preach the gospel, I have*
> *nothing to boast of, for necessity*
> *is laid upon me; yes, woe is me*
> *if I do not preach the gospel!*
> *— 1 Corinthians 9:16*

Give Me a Call!

We make contact with dozens of people every day — in person, by phone or through other communication. If you constantly think "good news," there will be natural opportunities for you to share it.

A man in Albuquerque told me that his evangelism is subtle but effective. Instead of blasting people out of the saddle with a Bible-thumping approach, after talking with a new acquaintance for a while, he simply states, "If you ever have a problem and you need someone to pray for you, give me a call."

He told me, "It's just amazing how many people I've eventually been able to help."

Look for every opportunity to share your faith — even if you have to sneeze to do it!

> *And He commanded us to preach*
> *to the people, and to testify that it is*
> *He who was ordained by God to be the*
> *Judge of the living and the dead.*
> *— Acts 10:42*

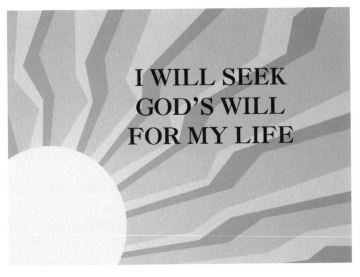

I WILL SEEK GOD'S WILL FOR MY LIFE

IN A REMOTE area of Liberia, I once visited the New Hope leper colony. One humid afternoon, I watched a nurse from New York wrap fresh bandages on the open ulcers of several patients in an outdoor clinic.

Later I asked her, "Don't you get discouraged having to deal with this horrible disease?"

"Not at all," she replied. "This is a joy for me. It's God's will for my life."

Her belief was much like that of the early missionary-explorer, David Livingstone, who said, "I would rather be in the heart of Africa in the will of God than on the throne of England out of the will of God."

A Vanishing Mist

We can design grand strategies and develop great schemes for our futures, but they are hollow unless they match the Father's plan. The apostle Paul wrote, "Now listen, you who say, 'Today or tomorrow we will go to this or that city, spend a year there, carry on business and make money.' Why, you do not even know what will happen tomorrow. What is your life? You are a mist that appears for a little while and then vanishes. Instead, you ought to say, 'If it is the Lord's will, we will live and do this or that.'" (James 4:13-15, NIV).

Peace in the Storm

Experiencing the will of the Almighty is like finding the eye of a hurricane. The storm may swirl around you, but in that center there is perfect peace and calm.

How can we discern the Lord's desire for our lives? Writer F. B. Meyer said, "When we want to know God's will, there are three things which always occur: 1) the inward impulse, 2) the Word of God and 3) the trend of circumstances." He added, "Never act until these things agree."

Remember, it is not *your* will but God's. Some people tell God, "Listen! Your servant is speaking." However, in the Old Testament, Samuel said to the Lord, "Speak, for your servant is listening" (1 Samuel 3:10, NIV).

If God can make trillions of snowflakes with no two formations alike, you can be assured that He has a unique plan and pattern for you.

When He speaks, listen. When He commands, obey. When He leads, follow.

And do not be conformed to this world,
but be transformed by the renewing of your
mind, that you may prove what is that good
and acceptable and perfect will of God.
— Romans 12:2

I VOW TO OBEY GOD'S COMMANDMENTS

I DON'T BELIEVE in the Ten Commandments," a young man in Canada flippantly announced. He was a passenger in a car being driven by an elderly minister.

"Why not?" the clergyman asked.

"Well, I don't like to constantly be told, 'Thou shalt,' or 'Thou shalt not,'" he replied.

When the minister came to the next intersection, he deliberately took the wrong road. The young man quickly raised his voice and warned, "Stop! You're headed in the wrong direction. The arrow pointed the other way to Toronto."

The senior minister smiled and replied, "I don't need some sign to tell me which way to go."

The young man got the point.

A Clear Command

For centuries governments and legislative bodies have attempted to improve on the standards of conduct God delivered to Moses at Mount Sinai. They have passed millions of laws but none as authoritative and clear as those carved on the original tablets of stone.

The editor of a West Texas newspaper had some space to fill so he printed the Ten Commandments without comment. Three days later he received a letter from a reader who wrote, "Cancel my subscription. You're getting too personal!"

Can They Be Kept?

The commandments of Scripture number far more than ten. According to *Dake's Annotated Reference Bible* there are 2,277 statutes embodied in the 445 laws of Moses and a surprising 1,050 commands in the New Testament for Christians to obey.

Keeping God's codes of conduct would be totally impossible unless we respond out of love instead of fear. There is one directive that, if accepted, will change your entire perspective. John, the disciple, wrote, "And this is his command: to believe in the name of his Son, Jesus Christ, and to love one another as he commanded us" (1 John 3:23, NIV).

Today, renew your vow to embrace God's laws of love.

He who has My commandments
and keeps them, it is he who loves
Me. And he who loves Me will be
loved by My Father, and I will love
him and manifest Myself to him.
— John 14:21

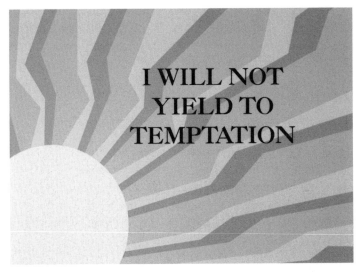

I WILL NOT
YIELD TO
TEMPTATION

I N A CRISIS on the Mississippi River, thousands of volunteers in a small Illinois community worked around the clock piling sandbags to keep their homes and fields from being flooded.

As the river was nearing its crest, there was one tiny hole in the levee where water came trickling through. By the time it was noticed, the small leak had become a torrent that submerged the small town and ruined the farmland.

The small weak spot in the floodwall is comparable to what happens when we yield to just one temptation. We say, "Oh, I can handle it." Then suddenly we are engulfed by events that leave us struggling for survival.

Should You Experiment?

I've met those who believe they need to try everything life has to offer before choosing their path. Art Linkletter addressed that issue when he commented, "Sometimes I'm asked by kids why I condemn marijuana when I haven't tried it. My answer is that the greatest obstetricians in the world have never been pregnant."

Others feel that because they are less than perfect there must be a flaw in their character. Bishop Fulton Sheen explained, "You are not tempted because you are evil; you are tempted because you are human."

The Lord knows you will be tested, and He is already preparing for your deliverance. Here is His promise:

> *No temptation has overtaken you except*
> *such as is common to man; but God is*
> *faithful, who will not allow you to be*
> *tempted beyond what you are able, but*
> *with the temptation will also make the way*
> *of escape, that you may be able to bear it.*
> *— 1 Corinthians 10:13*

The Test

You may be attracted by the lure, but it doesn't mean you have to take the bait. The words of Winston Churchill are still true: "Never give in, never, never, never, never — in nothing great or small, large or petty — never give in except to convictions of honor and good sense."

In the university of life you are being tested every day. Are you passing the exam?

> *Watch and pray, lest you enter*
> *into temptation. The spirit indeed*
> *is willing, but the flesh is weak.*
> *— Matthew 26:41*

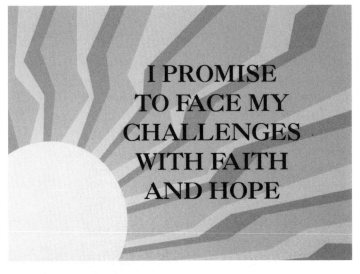

I PROMISE TO FACE MY CHALLENGES WITH FAITH AND HOPE

DON'T FRET ABOUT your problems. A diamond cannot be polished without friction, and you won't be perfected without trials.

A botanist will tell you that a giant oak tree needs the blustery March winds bending its branches. That's how its trunk and major limbs are flexed so that the sap is drawn up to feed the budding leaves.

We wish it were not true, but conflict is also necessary for our growth. A man who reached his one hundredth birthday was asked, "What is life's heaviest burden?" He thought for a moment and sadly answered, "Having nothing to carry."

From Beginning to End

Perhaps the most devastating word in the English language is *hopeless.* When that word is spoken by a medical doctor it causes emotional scars that are often more fatal than the disease itself.

God's Word is a book of hope because from beginning to end there are hundreds of stories of great belief and expectation — from Noah's faith to build the ark (Genesis 6) to our confidence that we will spend eternity with the Lord (Revelation 22).

When your faith includes the fact that you will someday face the Almighty and give an account for your life, your behavior suddenly changes. That is why Scripture proclaims:

> *And everyone who has this hope in Him*
> *purifies himself, just as He is pure.*
> *— 1 John 3:3*

Moving Mountains

It is not difficult to find people who believe in the power of positive expectation. In essence, they only have faith in faith. But I believe in placing our trust in a God who is real — who can move mountains on our behalf. Andrew Murray, the noted English minister, said, "Never try to arouse your faith from within. You cannot stir up faith from the depths of your heart. Leave your heart, and look into the face of Christ."

Allow the Lord to be the source of your hope.

> *Why are you cast down, O my soul?*
> *And why are you disquieted within me?*
> *Hope in God; for I shall yet praise Him,*
> *the help of my countenance and my God.*
> *— Psalm 42:11*

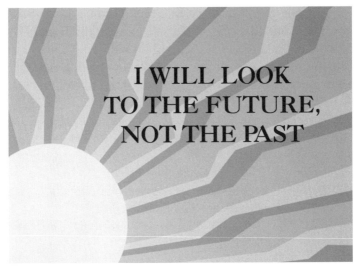

I WILL LOOK
TO THE FUTURE,
NOT THE PAST

HAVE YOU EVER encountered people who constantly yearn for the "good old days"? I bump into them often.

A man recently told me, "I can remember paying only eighteen cents a gallon for gas!"

I asked him, "Would you trade what you earned this year for your income that same year?"

"Well, I'd have to think about that," he responded.

Would we really like to return to the days of driving our cars in the scorching heat without air conditioning? Would we like to have a dentist drill our teeth without modern technology?

The Adventure Ahead

There is nothing wrong in remembering your past. It's your heritage, and it holds many treasured memories. Yesterday, however, is not where you want to live. As youth leader Mark Muirhead says, "The past is my history instructor. It's like a catapult that launches me to future adventures."

Believing that tomorrow will be better than today is an attitude worth adopting. It doesn't mean you will one day touch a computer button that will provide every answer or that hospital doors will be closed because all diseases have been cured. No, until we reach heaven there won't be perfection, but there will certainly be promise.

God created us with eyes that look forward because that is the direction He intends for us to travel. Jesus declared:

> *"No one, having put his hand*
> *to the plow, and looking back,*
> *is fit for the kingdom of God."*
> *— Luke 9:62*

Great Anticipation

Don't be a reactionary, only responding to events as they unfold. Anticipate the future, and take bold action.

One of the all-time great hockey players, Wayne Gretzky, was asked about his secret for leading the National Hockey League in goals year after year. Said Gretzky, "I skate to where the puck is going to be, not where it has been."

Every morning when you arise, thank God for the miracle called life. Rejoice in the present, and remember that the best is yet to come.

> *And let us not grow weary*
> *while doing good, for in due season*
> *we shall reap if we do not lose heart.*
> *— Galatians 6:9*

Promise #101

I PROMISE TO CELEBRATE GOD'S GOODNESS

STOP FOR A moment and take an inventory of your life. What are your assets? What are your liabilities? Somehow we have become like those who choose what stories will appear on page one of the morning paper. We concentrate on crisis and conflict, ignoring what is worth praising.

There are countless joys in our lives we take for granted — the love of our families, the concern of a friend, the challenge of our work and the protection of God's hand. These are priceless gifts. As the apostle Paul expressed:

Rejoice in the Lord always.
Again I will say, rejoice!
— Philippians 4:4

Giving Life

In his book, *The Star Thrower,* Loren Eisley tells the story of a man who lived near the sea. During the tourist season he watched shell collectors walk the beach at dawn gathering starfish, clams and sea urchins. Then they'd throw them in boiling pots the hotels provided, killing the shellfish and taking them as souvenirs.

This man walked along the shore, too. Only he didn't have a bag for his collection. Instead, he would pick up the living objects and fling them out to sea, just beyond the breaking surf.

One of the tourists walked over to the man and asked, "What are you doing?"

"I'm a star thrower," the man answered, picking up another starfish and tossing it back to the sea. "It may live if the offshore pull is strong enough."

He wasn't collecting; he was celebrating.

Worth Shouting About

The book of Psalms is the story of a dramatic transformation in the life of David. At the start he was watering his couch with his tears (Psalm 6:6). Then he states, "I waited patiently for the Lord; he turned to me and heard my cry" (Psalm 40:1, NIV).

God kept His promise to David, and he was able to say, "He alone is my rock and my salvation" (Psalm 62:2, NIV). How does the final psalm conclude? It is a festival of praise.

This book is not about promises worth making, but it's about promises worth *keeping*. Every vow you fulfill is a victory. Every commitment you complete is a triumph. This is not a time to weep, but it is a time to sing.

Start celebrating!

Let everything that has breath
praise the Lord. Praise the Lord!
— Psalm 150:6

OTHER BOOKS BY NEIL ESKELIN

Yes Yes Living in a No No World

The 24-Hour Turn-Around

*What to Do When You
Don't Know What to Do*

Powerful Principles for Personal Growth
(Also available in audio and video)

If you would like to purchase any of
the above titles, or to schedule the author
for speaking engagements, you may contact:

Neil Eskelin
Box 742812
Charlotte, NC 28247
FAX: (704) 846-8965

If you enjoyed *101 Promises Worth Keeping,* we would
like to recommend the following books:

Victory
by A. C. Green

NBA champion and all-star A. C. Green gives the scriptural
principles he has used to raise the standard of morality and
integrity as a professional athlete. His principles will help
you discover how to be a champion for God by living a
pure and moral life by boldly witnessing for the gospel.

Words of Promise
by John Mason and Tim Redmond

This collection of quotes is from more than one hundred
of today's leading Christian men. Men such as Billy
Graham, Chuck Swindoll and James Dobson will inspire
you to break down the barriers in your life to achieve
excellence and become all God wants you to be.

Strong Men in Tough Times
by Edwin Louis Cole

From the best-selling author of *Maximized Manhood*
comes the book for today's man. Men have lost the
meaning of manhood in their quest for self-gratification
with the world progressing technologically, but regress-
ing morally and spiritually. While the world looks for
better methods, God looks for better men.

Available at your local Christian bookstore or from:

Creation House
600 Rinehart Road
Lake Mary, FL 32746
1-800-283-8494